RECLAIMING
THE SOUL
OF
YOUR FAITH

RECLAIMING THE SOUL OF YOUR FAITH

Finding the vital elements of your own beliefs

Dr. Randolph W.B. Becker

The New Atlantian Library

The New Atlantian Library
is an imprint of
ABSOLUTELY AMAZING eBOOKS

Published by Whiz Bang LLC, 926 Truman Avenue, Key West, Florida 33040, USA

Reclaiming the Soul of Your Faith copyright © 2001 by Randolph W.B. Becker. Electronic compilation/paperback edition copyright © 2013 by Whiz Bang LLC.

All rights reserved. No part of this book may be reproduced, scanned, or transmitted in any form or by any means, electronic or mechanical, including photocopying, recording, or any information storage and retrieval system, without permission in writing from the publisher. Please do not participate in or encourage piracy of copyrighted materials in violation of the author's rights. Purchase only authorized ebook editions.

This work is based on factual events. While the author has made every effort to provide accurate information at the time of publication, neither the publisher nor the author assumes any responsibility for errors, or for changes that occur after publication. Further, the publisher does not have any control over and does not assume any responsibility for author or third-party websites or their contents.

Cover Photograph by Dr. Randolph W.B. Becker.

For information contact
Publisher@AbsolutelyAmazingEbooks.com
ISBN-13:978-0615919584
ISBN-10: 0615919588

RECLAIMING THE SOUL OF YOUR FAITH

TABLE OF CONTENTS

Introduction: **A CRITICAL EXAMINATION**

Chapter 1: **IS THIS REALLY "LIFE AS WE KNOW IT?"**

Chapter 2: **OPEN**
Inclusive vs. exclusive

Chapter 3: **CONNECTED**
Unifying vs. differentiating

Chapter 4: **UNITARY**
Unified vs. fragmented

Chapter 5: **HOPEFUL (progressive)**
Forward looking vs. backward looking

Chapter 6: **FREEING**
Liberating vs. confining

Chapter 7: **CONTEMPLATIVE**
Questions vs. answers

Chapter 8: **INDEPENDENT**
Influences institutions vs. being influenced by institutions of culture

Chapter 9: **CREATIVE**
active vs. static

Chapter 10: **ACCESSIBLE-REASONABLE**
Evident vs.
secret/mysterious

Chapter 11: **SPIRITUAL**
Spiritual vs. material

Chapter 12: **OUR PATHS INTO THE FUTURE**

Introduction

A CRITICAL EXAMINATION

Suppose that someone came into your home and took one of your prized possessions? What would you do?

Probably the answer depends on how soon you noticed the theft.

If you noticed it right away, you would probably call the police, call the insurance company, and then feel violated. You would hope you could get your prized thing back. And if you can't get it back, you hope that you can be reimbursed enough that you can replace it. But what if it is irreplaceable?

You might hope that whoever took it will be caught and properly punished. You will probably hope that you can overcome the feeling of violation which leaves you feeling a little unsafe even in your own home.

In the process you may make some changes in your living and your thinking. You might decide to increase security in your home. You might increase your insurance. You might re-evaluate what is of value to you, what you want to keep, what you are willing to treasure, what you are willing to lose. Life, in a sense, will never be the same again because of this event.

But, what if you didn't notice right away? What if you came home, did not notice your treasure was gone, and went on with your life? It is possible you would never notice the loss. But more likely, a day will come when you go looking for the thing out of some need, and you will not find it. What then?

Most people will assume they will have lost it? (I mean both lost the object and "lost it.") It must be around somewhere, but where was it put?

Some people will assume that someone borrowed it.

Some people will assume that it has been inadvertently thrown out.

And some, a very few, will come to the conclusion that a theft has taken place.

But when? By whom? Is anything else missing? What to do now?

What would you do if you came to the conclusion that someone had taken something of value to you, without your noticing, some time in the past?

(And what if you also came to the conclusion that the "someone" was a person you knew, a person you trusted?)

Either way, you would be in a "crisis."

What had been "known and given" is now no longer "known and given."

You will be called upon to re-evaluate many things – your sense of self, the things you value, your sense of security, and perhaps your relationship to someone else.

This would become a time of "critical examination", when you would be forced to examine many things because of this crisis.

Whether discovered sooner or later, such a loss would mean that you would need to ask yourself lots of questions. Tough questions.

OK. Now what if I told you that someone had stolen your faith?

I think this is the truth for most people.

Usually slowly, and unnoticed, the theft has taken place.

Few people are abducted by some sect which steals their previous faith and substitutes a new one in its place.

Most of us pass through life in less extreme ways.

But, as I will suggest in Chapter 1, I think you know that a theft has taken place.

You may not have reached a crisis point yet, but many people have.

Witness the present rise in conversions from "mainline" religious traditions into more diverse religious groups.

Witness the impressive growth in the religious publishing business as people read more about faith than ever before.

Witness the appearance of the "new age" movement with its own spiritual representation of traditionally religious concerns.

Witness the many, many spiritual self-help programs, tapes, website, books, and speakers.

Many people have gone looking for that valued treasure, their faith, and found that it has been taken.

Unfortunately, this usually happens at a time when they need that faith in some ultimate way. Loss, change, grief, doubt, fear – life's events of turmoil send them looking for that faith which they have assumed was always safely tucked away ... and they find only an empty shell, a pilfered box, a drained chalice of faith.

In the aftermath of both the precipitating event and the awful discovery of the loss, people feel adrift, alone, violated ... and there is no faith police and no faith insurance. In fact, their faith was supposed to be their insurance.

These people have been forced into a critical examination by the circumstances of life.

And that has made the discovery of the theft of their faith doubly hard. Just when they needed it most, they found it was gone.

Do you want that to happen to you?

If not, then I suggest that you engage in a critical examination of your faith without the pressures of an actual crisis. I invite you to an in-depth examination of key elements of faith that will not only help you assess the power and meaning of your faith, but it will also help protect your faith from theft by anyone.

And if, in the process, you discover the sad truth that too many people only realize in times of crisis – that your faith has been stolen, or rendered lifeless, or replaced with someone else's faith – this process of examination will help you lay claim once again to those things which speak intimately to your spirit from the infinite possibility of the universe.

As well, you may find that your faith has not been stolen but has been neglected, untended, or under-nourished.

Or maybe your faith has been ignored because you feared investing in it, lest it be stolen.

Come, my friends ... don't wait for a crisis.

Let's do this examination together so

YOU CAN RECLAIM THE SOUL OF YOUR FAITH!

Chapter 1
IS THIS REALLY "LIFE AS WE KNOW IT?"

Does the world make sense to you?
Or rather, does the world you have been told to believe in make sense to you?
If you answer "No", then you are in company with the majority of people today.
Most people I talk with have either a clear sense or a sneaking suspicion that they are being fed a line when it comes to understanding such primary concepts as:

>the meaning of life
>the nature of reality
>the sources of knowledge
>   and understanding.

The things that most people were taught in their childhood, no matter what their religious or ethnic persuasion, now appear to leave them with more questions unanswered than answered. Over and over again, people come to me saying, "I know I was taught this, but it just doesn't make sense." Have you ever said that yourself?

In coming to me, a religious professional, these people then ask me to help them with a task: helping them make sense out of what they have been taught. They believe that they are the ones who are "out -of-whack" and that what was taught to them is still true, foundational, valid.

My reaction is to ask them to describe their life, as they know it. Not as it is described by some philosophy, some theology, some abstraction, but as they know it. I want to hear what they have to say about being alive, about trying to make meaning in the process of life, about the joys and sorrows of life, about their values and their dreams.

What would you tell me about your life? About life **as you know it**?

- - -

Let me tell you about life **as I know it**. See if you see your response echoed in my reflections.

I experience that I was born out of mystery. As unseen as that time before my being is, I sense that I arrived in this physical realm as:

> something more than a chemical statistical probability;
> something more than a biological being;
> something more than a participant in a single spiritual journey from birth to death;
> **something more than a cluster of physical and psychological**
>   traits;
> something more than the whimsical product of divine fancy.

My experiences in life lead me to "know" that I had some existence prior to this physical one. This is not the only life path I have or will trod.

At the other end of this physical existence, as unseen as that time beyond appears to be, I sense that:

> There is a continuity of some sense of my self that is more than simply memories held by people who knew me;

whatever lies beyond is as organic and dynamic as is this physical life (we do not stop growing and developing in death);

all of the words and symbols we have now are inadequate to fully capture the realities of what lies beyond life.

In the time between birth and death, here is some of what I observe about life, **as I know it**:

despite well-publicized acts of violence existent in all cultures, I find that people are by their basic nature: good, kind, and caring;

the prevailing systems of thought, organization, and action (religious, political, economic) fail to build on that basic human nature, and encourage us rather to behavior which is: competitive, violent, malicious, and uncaring.

Does this describe life **as you know it**?

Well, when I ask those who come to me for counseling on the conflict between what they have been taught and what they know from their life experience, they tell me the same things from their lives that I have experienced in mine.

They sense a meaning to life that is larger than either a scientific or a religious interpretation, the one being limited to empirical evidence and the other often being limited to individualized or single-shot salvation.

They sense a meaning to life that is more humane that either a political or an economic interpretation, the one being limited to the acquisition and control of systems of power and the other to the manipulation of resources for the limited benefit of some.

They sense that all human being have a potential for goodness and meaning far beyond what any of these disciplines describe or encourage. They sense that all the great teachers of humanity have caught a glimpse of that potential and have tried to transmit that glimpse to the larger community. They sense there is more meaning and understanding than what is sealed within the already proclaimed scientific, political, faith, and economic theories of the world.

Much of their apprehension of this comes from their experience of a dissonance between what they are told and what they know from their own living.

Listen to these comments:

In my work, in research, I know that I need to stay factual, to follow the measurements. But, when I am holding my daughter in my arms I know there are things that can't be measured - does that mean they are not real?

I sit in services each week, and I hear about sins, and I think to myself, sure, I've made mistakes, but those mistakes do not define who I am; in fact, they are more markers on my path to who I am becoming, as I step away from them. Yet, every week, every goddamn week, I am told that I am basically sinful. Well, either the preacher or I am wrong here - and I tend to trust my own experiences.

They come by here every four years - come by with banners and promises - and they shout at us about how they are going to build us a great new city, if only we would vote for them. Then, for four years the only time we hear about them is when they are debating somebody else's business.

This plant was never very large, but we always turned out good products. Sure, I'll admit it, it could have been done cheaper somewhere else, but not better, not even as good. Maybe our profit was only 3%, but to me, this job was 100% of my life. Now they got my 100% and their 3% and I got nothing. It wasn't like I was asking for a handout, I still made them money just not the money they wanted.

Does any of this match life **as you know it**?

My second question to those who come to me (after I ask them to describe life as they know it) is: **how would you like life to be?**

So, **how would YOU like life to be?**

- - -

At first I expected certain answers would pour out:

    I want to be richer.

    I want life to be easier.

In fact, those are not the answers I get (except for the occasional joke, followed by a prompt, "But, no, seriously...."). The people who come to me want things that are much more important to them than money and material possession, and they are willing to work hard to get them.

They describe a constellation of qualities of life, and they comment on how they find these qualities lacking in life as they know it.

They tell me the life they desire would be:

Open - that life can be explored with fewer artificial boundaries.

Connected - that there is a sense of connection that links them with others.

Unitary - that those links express a unity about all existence as experienced in life, work, meaning.

Hopeful - that the unity of life contains an element of hope that illumines a progressive belief that things can and will continue to evolve toward goodness.

Freeing - that such hope, while calling for individual and collective effort, is ultimately liberating in moving us beyond limitations of the various forms of fear.

Contemplative - that the human capacity to always have more questions than answers will then be free to help us explore the hopeful possibilities beyond our present knowing.

Independent - that the free human spirit will serve its own quest for meaning more than it will serve institutions of other times, other circumstances, other people.

Creative - that such a free life will be organic, finding its own evolving path as a living expression of creation.

Reasonable - that what is creatively discovered along the way will be known by us because it is accessible to all in easily understood terms.

Spiritual - that what we come to know and understand will fulfill us spiritually, making us feel whole and full.

Life would be open, connected, unitary, hopeful, freeing, contemplative, independent, creative, reasonable, and spiritual.

That is what people have told me **the life they desire would be!**

> **Open**
>   **Connected**
>   **Unitary**
>   **Hopeful**
>   **Freeing**
>   **Contemplative**
>   **Independent**
>   **Creative**
>   **Reasonable**
>   **Spiritual**

Does this list include your wishes for how the life you desire would be? (In spirit, if not in specific words)

Not surprisingly, these values form the core of a human longing, a longing as old as recorded human history. The origins of most religious and social traditions are found in that longing. Ask yourself, from the perspective of the tradition of your upbringing, were these not the goals of that tradition when it was founded?

But, if that is true, why do so many people come to my door asking for help to reconcile life as they know it and the current practices of those traditions?

I think it is because almost all (if not all) of our major world social and religious traditions have lost their souls! Where they once sought to break barriers,
> now they erect and vehemently maintain them.

Where people once found new connection through more universal ideas,
> now there is separation.

Where once there was a drive to unify different people and ideas,
> now there is differentiation.

Where messages of hope once prevailed,
> now messages of fear abound.

Where the individual once found freedom,
> now she or he finds obligation and obedience.

Where there were once questions,
> now there are answers, and often dogmatic answers.

Where institutions once arose to express the insights of the people,
> now the people are asked to serve the empty warehouses of those institutions.

Where once new ideas were welcomed as expressions of the on-going reality of creation,
> now ideas are treated with suspicion, fear, and anger.

Where new insights were once evident to the people,
> now the policies are written by people isolated from life's realities, composed in language inaccessible to the common person, and seemingly irrelevant to everyday life.

Where once spiritual issues and values predominated,
 now re-election, building drives, and institutional security and survival are paramount concerns.
 Whatever soul our social and religious traditions had, it is lost.
 And it is not that we, the people, lost it. We have always been seeking it.
 When it was alive for us, we knew it.
 Now that it is gone, we again seek it!

 So, if **life as YOU know it *is not* life as YOU think it could be**
 and
 you think life could be open, connected, unitary, hopeful, freeing, contemplative, independent, creative, reasonable, and spiritual

Let's see how we can identify the loss of the soul of our collective faith and
explore some new ways to restore the soul of our collective faith that we all seek.
Come, let's explore together.

Chapter 2

OPEN
INCLUSIVE versus EXCLUSIVE

A few years ago I sent for a brochure of a specific hotel on a resort lake. I was delighted when I read about the property and saw the pictures. The "lakeside" hotel boasted of a tranquil garden with panoramic views of the lake and the mountains opposite. The view from the dining room windows was across this garden, was "of an equally impressive nature." The hotel, in picture and in description was a Victorian structure with balconies, high ceilings, awnings. In a word, "*Magnifique!*"

When we arrived at the hotel, we began to see that we had been given only a piece of the picture. The front of the hotel did indeed have the garden, but the arrival was to an entrance barely 2 meters from a busy thoroughfare. The main building was Victorian, but the wing of our room was more 1960s. The garden overlooked the lake, and overlooked a very busy pedestrian walkway, whose occupants could and did look over those of us in the garden. The tranquility of the garden was disturbed a bit by the frequent passage of trains on the mainline about 100 meters away, along but above that busy thorough-fare. And as for the view from the dining room; had the blinds, needed against the afternoon sun, been opened there might have been a great view.

That little brochure tried to capture a broad picture and condense it down to a few choice words with well-placed and cropped pictures. It was certainly more exclusive than inclusive in its information.

(Now, I need to quickly add that the lake itself was shining elegance, the fresh breezes coming into our room exhilarating, and the down beds almost heavenly. It would have been too easy to sink into the exclusive view of these things and miss the larger picture.)

The brochure, by being exclusive in its information, was not very open. It presented a closed view of reality.

I have also been an invitee to many social gatherings. Some I know will be exclusive, because they have been announced with a specific intention. But there are others which are announced as open events; I attend these thinking that I will find my style, thoughts, and needs reflected in some of the others in attendance. I think of one particular evening when I was invited to an "Event of the Arts". While not a connoisseur of the arts, I am deeply moved by a great variety of artistic expression. I went with high hopes that some of the evening would touch me. Imagine how I felt when the "art" of the evening turned out to be a lengthy performance of an amateur jazz performance of enthusiastic but not overly gifted players. "Art" had been reduced down to a very small, exclusive meaning. This was a closed gathering around a not very open understanding of art.

We experience this all of the time.

The menu claims "seafood" but only lists fish sticks.

The buffet claims 46 items, 8 of them different flavors of Jell-O™.

The invitation said, "Come as you are" and you don't

believe everyone else was already wearing formal wear.

The advertisement said "All services included" and you are billed $29 for services not included.

But we also experience this in more serious ways.

Most of the religions of the world offer us an exclusive view.

A subtext to almost any religious pronouncement is "We are right - they are wrong."

Universals are reduced to specifics, and those specific are made exclusive.

I would represent this as:

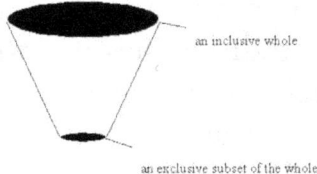

First of all, if we conceive that all-that-is (what is known by many as God, or Allah) as an infinite source of creation and meaning, we could never draw the inclusive circle big enough to include it all. Every attempt of finite humanity to create a circle that large would result automatically in an exclusive subset of the whole. Only if we were all-that-is would we be capable of describing and containing the infinite scope of the universal. We would need to be as Gods ourselves to be able to include the totality of the divine.

So, we start from a position of exclusivity. What we can include in our own version of the universe is already limited by our human limitations.

Reclaiming the Sould of Your Faith

Yet, for most of us humans, we have some shared vision of what would be in the most inclusive circle we could draw. Those qualities have been contained in the sacred thinking of the great religious leaders: love, acceptance, forgiveness, empathy, compassion, justice, equity, human potential, human goodness ... what qualities would you add to the list, that you think all people would accept?

- - -

But, as we know, most religious traditions take those qualities, and place restrictions on them. We are told that some exclusive subset of those qualities is what is actually true. Each religious tradition has its own formula of how much of which is included in its smaller circle.

Yet, the result is always the same. A smaller circle is being projected *as if it were the same as the larger, more universal, more inclusive circle.*

It is as if a religion, in having defined the exclusive, reduced circle of specifics it claims to be the sum of truth and understanding, then uses that circle like a slide in a slide projector, and the image of that limited circle projected outward is said to be all of reality.

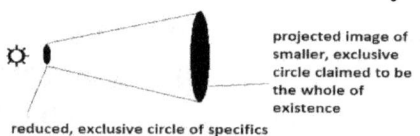

And the smaller circle is a closed circle! That is, what is included in that smaller circle is decided by someone other than you! And there is no room for adding anything more or other! So, the larger circle projected as if it were the whole is also a closed circle, with no room for anything to be added, no room for anything new.

A piece of all-that-is is passed off as being the whole picture, and nothing that has been excluded from the smaller circle will be allowed in. This is the theological circle, a definition of truth and meaning that limits what is acceptable belief and knowledge, and clearly states what is not. Some person, or group of persons, claims to have the truth, and that truth includes only some of all-that-is, and excludes much of all-that-is.

This is one of the signs of that we are not dealing with life as we know it could be.

When we are asked to accept a piece of the picture as the whole picture, and also are told that nothing can or will be added, this is not as we know it could be.

The first sign we can be looking for as we seek the new renewal of the soul of our collective faith is whether we are dealing with ever more expansive or ever more restrictive views of life. Are we being encouraged to look for the largest circle possible, or are we told we must settle for a smaller version?

A faith that is open to the thoughts and interpretations of all others will also be open to ours!

Poet Edwin Markham wrote:

> *He drew a circle that shut me out*
> *Heretic, rebel, a thing to flout*
> *But love and I had the wit to win*
> *We drew a circle that took him in.*

The circle may be closed in its content, but it may also

be closed in terms of participation. Most religious traditions have very definite rules for who is within their circle and who is not. The defining quality may be specific beliefs, or it may be salvation, or it may be tribal lineage, or it may be certain knowledge, or it may be the extent of one's gifts to the tradition, or it may be participation in defined practices.

Whatever the defining quality, the circle of participation is seen as a group smaller than the whole of humanity, often much smaller. There is an exclusive set of people who are counted as religious, and the rest are excluded.

In other words, such a religious circle of participation (as opposed to the theological circle of beliefs/truths) is closed. It is not open to many people in life as they know it. At the present time, there is no major religious tradition whose circle is open to all the people of the earth as they are.

This is another of the signs of that we are not dealing with life as we know it could be.

At the present time, with the advances of global communications, we are sensing more intensely the common fate of all humanity. The ideals which we seek are ideals for all of humanity. Our hope is for a world in which we do not have to think in terms of "us" and "them", but rather of "we". This is a global extension of the American sense of "We, the people...."

In a more perfect world, the circles of inclusion would

always be in the process of expansion, always seeking to include more, and exclude fewer people. The edges of the circle would be porous points of inclusion, not sealed fortresses of exclusion.

The second sign we can be looking for as we seek this new renewal of the soul of our collective faith is that we are dealing with ever more expansive rather than ever more restrictive systems for including people. Are we talking about all of humanity or something less?

A faith that is open to all other people will also be open to us!

Whether it is a matter of content or participation, the path to the creation of a soulful shared faith has always been the same: to find and create a larger, more inclusive, more open circle.

The great Buddha encouraged people from diverse ethnic and religious traditions to envision a universal spirit, in which all existence participates.

Moses, the great leader, helped to unify disparate tribes into a nation around the concept of a central, inclusive faith.

The message of Jesus quickly spread through a variety of religious and ethnic identities because his words pointed to a divine spirit that embraced them all, not just some.

For the oft-warring, yet culturally sophisticated tribes of the Arabic world, Mohammed's vision drew them into a spiritual unity which could transcend their differences.

Sadly, each of these roots of inclusivity has been used as the foundation to create theologies and theocracies of exclusion. Too soon radical words of inclusion are forgotten in the rush to create institutions, security, doctrine. We remember the names of the Buddha, Moses, Jesus, and Mohammed more than we remember their message. Recorded scripture or ritualized practice replaces intimate interaction with and personal implementation of the themes of inclusivity they each preached **and** practiced.

The preachers and speakers and writers,
the artists and composers and poets,
the thinkers and planners and designers,
of life as it could be
will tell us, show us, create for us systems of thought that are
open to growth, open to development, open to being inclusive in content
and open to all people, open to all cultures, open to being inclusive in participation.

If anyone shares with you a vision that is not open in this way, it will not lead to life as you know it can be.

This is the first test of our faiths, as they are now,
and
this is the first criterion of the collective faith we wish to create and sustain:

Is this a model or mode that leads us to be radically open in thought, interaction, and participation?

Are we being asked to include or exclude ideas and people?

Chapter 3
CONNECTED
UNIFYING versus DIFFERENTIATING

Think about the way that you live out your life.
What is one of the strongest forces in human life for most people? As social animals, we are drawn to connect to others. We sense innately that none of us is sufficient, in and of ourselves alone, to all the tasks of living. We sense even before we know that we must rely on others.

This lesson is learned in the earliest stages of our being physical, in the womb, in the caring arms of those who nurture us after birth, at the table of foods set before us through the efforts of others, in the rooms of learning where wisdom is shared with us, and so many other places of connection.

The ancient myth of Rome was that it was founded by the twins, Romulus and Remus, who had been abandoned but were nursed by a she-wolf. Not even these great builders of civilization nor that great civilization could make it alone.

Yet, almost at the same time that we are learning about our innate connectivity, we are being taught lessons to the contrary. Think for yourself when you first learned:
> that some things "belonged" to other people?
> that some people were "different" than you were?
> that you could not trust certain people?
> that you could not go to certain places, or play with certain people?

When did you first learn about the inherited (as opposed to innate) tendency of human beings to differentiate themselves?

What lessons were you taught?

Who taught you those lessons?

Why do you think they taught them to you?

- - - -

What comes to my mind is a simple contrast, but again something simple which has complex implications.

Is this an existence of plenty, or an existence of want?

Of course, many would answer that it depends on where you are and who you are. If we think only about material objects, that is probably true. The typical (or typified) household in the United States abounds with objects, while the typical (or typified) household in third world countries is barren of material goods.

If one goes to bed starving, then there is little question in my mind how one would view the world, as a world of want. But, what about those who go to bed not getting the desired dinner out at a favorite fast-food restaurant, having to "make-do" with homemade leftovers, and viewing their world as a world of want? There is a world of difference between the circumstances of those two people, but the result is still the same.

Either by circumstances or attitude or values, some people view life as an encounter with scarcity. They feel that their needs are not being met, much less their wants. They view the resources at hand as limited. There is only one pie, and if someone else gets more than his or her share, I will get that much less.

I know I have experienced this feeling, literally watching a family pie being cut into portions, knowing that some at the table do not like this type of pie but will take a full portion only to push it around the plate while my mouth waters for as much of it as I can get. If I give into my feelings of scarcity, I begin to look upon the others at the table as my rivals, even my enemies. I begin to see them as "other", for they are not my compatriots in enjoying this pie.

Have you ever experienced feelings like this?

Have you ever felt anger or jealousy toward someone else because you perceived that they were about to get what you felt you wanted, that you felt you needed?

What did that do to any bonds of connection you had previously enjoyed?

Scarcity thinking results in seeing others as competitors for the same scant resources.

And if others are competitors, then our brains tell us that we need to differentiate ourselves from them.

We need to be able to see them as "other".

Of course, adults showing us our way as children did not convey this message consciously. They instead transmitted personal and cultural perceptions which they had formed when they were taught by previous generations.

A single unshared cookie of one generation can easily become all-out warfare in some future generation when scarcity becomes the motif of thinking. With scarcity thinking, no slight is ever forgotten, no advantage ever forgiven, no commonality sought or desired.

Scarcity thinking thwarts our innate drive for connection.

But, what is the alternative?

For an answer I turn to those who seemingly have little. Our two younger daughters had the opportunity to travel to two different developing nations. In each case, they lived for several weeks on very limited diets, slept in rooms with dirt floors, had minimal hygiene facilities (as compared to United States standards), with electric lights, TVs, running water, and easy cooking in short supply.

What did they find?

People with intense senses of scarcity?

Quite the contrary!

They found people who had an expressed love of others and life, many social experiences, and a lively inclusion of music.

How was this possible?

These people had learned, probably through their religious faith, in a world of abundance.

Abundance of what?

Abundance of love, abundance of connection, abundance of possibility.

Abundance of all creation.

What does a view of abundance mean to a person?

In concrete terms, it means that when that pie comes out, and I see it being cut into pieces, I do not worry about what the others at the table will do with their portion. I think instead about how much I enjoy my piece, and how I can look forward to more of that pie in the future. I do not need to control the *now* in fear of a lack *then*. I can look around the table and see the people who share my meal as participants in a shared event, not as competitors for what I want or need.

Yet, many would say quickly, "but our resources are limited."

What resources?

When the Irish potato famine was at its peak, vast quantities of foodstuffs were being exported from Ireland to England. The resources were not limited, only hoarded.

When the people of California suffered their rolling blackouts, there was not a universal shortage of electricity, only distribution, profit, and use issues.

But, what of the less material resources?

When some people experience a lack of love in their families of origin, the universe is still over-flowing with a sense of love (which goes by the name of "creation"), a problem of focus not availability.

When others experience a scarcity of hope, there are often many beneficial outcomes to the situation although the desired one may be missing, again raising the issue of focus, not abundance.

It may appear that there are limited resources in a given moment, from a given perspective, with a given focus on specific wants and needs. This is like looking at a great beach with miles of golden sand through a telescope, looking to find a place to put down one's towel and enjoy the shore. Looking only at the small window provided by the telescope, one may only see people already occupying the sand. That kind of looking (and thinking) leads us to think that beach space is scarce, when in fact, the vast beach may be extremely abundant.

If you believe, as I do, in an infinite creation, a vast universe founded on the nurturing principle of love, then the beach is eternally, infinitely abundant even if my own view shows limitation and scarcity.

Once one embraces abundance as the underlying theme of the universe, even when one is not experiencing it in one's own immediate situation, many things change.

Abundance thinking breeds abundance. No, I am not talking about the positive-thought-brings -material-gain type of abundance. Rather, I am thinking in terms of the way in which our view changes as we open our eyes to the wider possibility. Even in the most limited vision, around the edges we sense possibility that is more felt than seen. As we open ourselves to those possibilities, then around the now wider perspective new edges are sensed full of possibility.

Just as scarcity thinking encourages an ever-narrower field of view, until only one's own needs and resources are seen in focus (and often even that is distorted), abundance thinking encourages an ever-wider field of view, until one's own needs and resources are dissolved in the larger reality of first community, then of humanity, then of the universe itself.

The barriers to connections fall down.

Others are not seen in a competitive mode.

And that change is vital in our reclaiming of our innate social nature.

Once we live in an abundance mode, we are then freed to make connections into ever-larger social units. We can find the inter-connections that allow us to feel that all of our wants and needs, especially those that we sense we cannot meet for ourselves, can be met in this social fabric.

Think of the joy and freedom of this!

First of all, think how wonderful, how joyous it would be to no longer live in fear and competition with others.

And think of how freeing it would be to live life open, not guarded.

The conversation at dessert time around my table can be enjoyed when I no longer worry about the distribution of the pie. It feels wonderful to be free to enjoy the other people and my connection to them.

Abundance, not scarcity.

- - - -

Now, with our minds and spirits tending toward abundance, let's return to the main theme of this chapter: *Connected:* Unifying Versus Differentiating.

Why connect?

Why make this an essential part of the emergent (or reclaimed) spirit of religion?

First, it expresses our innate nature as social, human beings. When we connect, we are being more truly at the heart of ourselves, freed of the learned lessons of separation. We are unlocking potential rather than closing ourselves in.

And we are reinforcing the concept of abundance.

This is an essential chicken-and-egg combination. We become more of ourselves when we think abundantly, and when we open ourselves to our connectional selves, we find more abundance.

But, how are we to know that we are moving in the direction of these oh-so-vital connections, into that abundance? I think a return to the beach can help us think about this.

What is a beach?

Some would say that a beach is the portion of land that lies beside a body of water.

But wait, that is speaking of two distinct components, land and water, the one the beach and the other the water.

Yet, you cannot have a beach without the water. So maybe the beach is the water and the land.

That's seeing the whole, the unity of the area.

Some others would point out that neither the land nor the water exist in isolation. The land is part of the *terra firma* that rises up out of the water, and the water is a product of a complex set of springs, streams, rivers, oceans. So, the beach is connected to all land and all waters.

Some others would then point to the planet as a whole, of which the beach is only a part, just as the planet is only a piece of the solar system, and then of the universe.

Unifying thinking.

By contrast, some others would argue that the water is inconsequential. The point is the land, and not just the land but the composition of the land. Some geologists would claim that a strip of sand isolated from any water can still be considered a beach, because sand only arises from the action of water at some time of the past.

But, what sand?

One cannot speak of the beach without speaking of the composition of the beach, and hence of the sand itself. What is the nature of the sand? And so a grain of sand is seen as the unit of focus.

But, what makes that grain of sand? And so on, to the molecules, to the atoms, to the sub-atomic particles. Until at last, the smallest unit is sought and determined. The whole is lost in search of the particular.

Yes, I know, by looking at the building blocks of the universe, we may also be looking for and at an underlying unity. Einstein, in looking to both the grand and the minute, sought a unified theory to explain all. The trick is to be sure one is seeking the all in the small, and not the less in the least.

I am reminded of William Blake's words:

To see a world in a grain of sand,
And a heaven in a wild flower,
Hold infinity in the palm of your hand
And eternity in an hour.

How, then, does this work out in our religious or spiritual life?

Most of modern religion is based on the differentiating mode.

While most religions speak of a universal divine presence, they almost immediately make that presence less than universal.

Think of the divisions about relatively minor points of theology that define all of the Protestant Christian denominations:

> Corporal vs. symbolic vs. memorial communion.
> Trespassers vs. debtors.
> Adult baptism, child baptism, full immersion baptism.

Reclaiming the Sould of Your Faith

Add into the equation the divisions between Protestant, Catholic, and Orthodox Christians, and all their differences.

And then consider Judaism and Islam, both growing from some of the same roots as Christianity.

Then, what of Buddhism, Hinduism, Taoism, Shinto?

And spiritualism, magic, wicca, animism?

Our many religious traditions are based on theories of differentiation, not unity.

They gain their significance not by participating in a perceived unity, but rather by promoting a specific certainty, a clear differentiation.

What does all of this have to do with you, with me?

I am not suggesting that any of us give up our personal religious connections.

Rather I want to suggest that if we want to renew the soul of our faith, we need to stop focusing on those elements which differentiate us from others, and start to look for those things which unify us with others.

We know we are doing this when we find that we see our particular points of belief and faith as parts of a larger unity, rather than a defining points over-and-against anyone.

> We know we are doing this when we listen to others share their faith and hear more points of agreement than points of argument.
>
> We know we are doing this when we stop speaking of "The Truth", and speak instead of "my understanding."
>
> We know we are doing this when we no longer feel defensive when we hear a divergent view.

We know we are doing this when we invite others to discuss rather than debate.

We know we are doing this when we can, in the presence of a larger unity, relinquish our former beliefs in favor of a greater understanding.

We know we are doing this when we sense we are moving, spiritually and religiously, and not just standing still, or even retreating.

This is the second test of our faiths, as they are now,
and
this is the second criterion of the collective faith we wish to create and sustain:

Is this a model or mode that leads us toward unity, connecting us to a larger whole?

Are we being asked to understand in ways that are narrower or wider?

Chapter 4
UNITARY
UNIFIED vs. FRAGMENTED

The other day I was having a discussion with an acquaintance when I was startled into paying more attention by the comment, "but that is not part of what I want to talk about." I had to recall what I had just said to see what was being labeled as foreign to the conversation. I was surprised that something I saw as germane to the discussion was so easily dismissed.

Yet, this happens all the time.

A Cabinet Minister issues a press release saying that he or she will no longer comment on certain ideas which are considered outside the vision of the administration.

An Internet message board moderator removes a string of discussion, not because it is obscene or slanderous or commercial, but because "it does not reflect the intent of this message board."

A teacher in a grade school responds to a student's answer by saying that "No, that's not what I was looking for."

Competing teams of high-energy physicists denigrate the findings of each other as irrelevant to the real solution.

A medium discounts the channeling by another medium.

And even your gourmand parent wonders why you

brought *that* dish to share at a recent family dinner.

Do these situations remind you of any in your own life?
What happened?
Were you the one shutting out someone or something else, or were you the one shut out?
How did it seem to you?
What was going on?

Let's look at each of these situations, and see if we can discover another lesson about our recovering the soul of our faith.

First, note that all of these situations involve people who have adopted some level of connection.

They are, at heart, promoting a unifying notion.

The adventuresome parental chef likes to explore and include new dishes in the menu.

The psychic looks to move beyond the limiting circles of the material world to include other notions of existence.

The scientific researchers all seek new, more inclusive understandings of the nature of things.

The teacher tries to open the students' minds to the larger world of ideas, knowledge, wisdom, and understanding.

The Internet website attempts to provide a venue for discussions and relationships which might not happen in one's everyday life situation.

The administration strives to find a new consensus that will allow it to better serve a wider range of its constituents.

My friend likes to experience interaction with new

ideas, connecting outside of self to a larger world of thought.

You, if you have read this far in this book, open yourself to expanding your horizons and finding connections.

None of these people, including you, is operating out of a sense of scarcity.

All have a sense of abundance.

All are moving through a series of connections.

All are generally welcoming, open.

But still, something is happening here, something else.

It is as simple as the difference between *this or that* and *this and that*.

It is the next step in our progression, through openness and through connection.

Let's see how it is and is not revealed in each of the situations I have mentioned.

> My friend, trying to be open to new ideas and generally seeking connection, made a judgment about whether a certain thing I said was within the conversation or outside of it.
>
> The Cabinet Minister, trying to find new solutions and a wider appeal, made a judgment that certain ideas would not help that process.
>
> The teacher, trying to open the students to unexplored concepts, made a judgment that a certain answer would impede that exploration.
>
> The physicists, trying to unlock the undiscovered secrets of creation, made a judgment that certain approaches would not provide the key.
>
> The medium, trying to be in communication with

spirit, made a judgment that certain claims to spirit were less reliable.

And your parent, always trying to assemble a table to explore palatable delights, made a judgment that a certain dish would violate the spirit of good taste.

Each one, trying to be open in wider and wider ways, made a judgment that something specific, some certain thing, did not fit, did not belong.

And what about you and your own situations? Despite a commitment to openness and connection, was there a judgment made?

Did you or someone else judge something specific, some certain thing, to be outside, unhelpful, impeding, useless, unreliable, a violation?

What does such a response represent?

To me, this is what I call "splinter thinking."

You remember splinters, don't you? In the world of my childhood, a world mainly built out of wood, we often got splinters, those small slivers of wood grain which separated from the whole.

They were pesky things. They hurt! And unattended, they could fester into an infection. But, removing them was as painful as keeping them (or so it seemed).

Once we got a sliver, that piece of the whole took on the aspect of something as large as, or even larger than the whole.

One might come home from a baseball game, and when asked about the game reply, "It was OK, but I got this sliver from the bleachers."

Now, why do I recall those slivers here?

Because when we move along the process through openness and connection, it is very easy to be taken by a sliver of this or that. A small piece of the grain of the whole catches onto and into us, and in the process we lose sight of the whole.

But, before saying more about "sliver thinking" I invite you to join me in exploring the "sight of the whole" for a while.

- - - -

I like to use the term "all-that-is" to describe the totality of existence. Even the word universe seems too small, as physically defined as it often is. All-that-is represents the same concept as God, Allah, Being, Spirit may mean to others.

Now, a question for you.

Can you think of anything which is not included in all-that-is?

This is the equivalent of asking you to think about something that is not natural.

> If it exists, it is natural.
> If it exists, it is part of all-that-is.
> If it ever existed, it is part of all-that-is.
> If it will ever exist, it is part of all-that-is.

This view is support by Stephen Hawking, the brilliant theoretical mathematician. In the on-going search for a unified theory which connects all-that-is in a consistent, understandable way, Hawking proposes that the smallest, *the smallest* unit we can consider is the whole of the universe, or all-that-is, if you will.

Everything else is only a part, a portion, of that essential unity.

Anything else, no matter how whole it may seem, is only a splinter, a piece of the grain of the whole.

And it is only in the whole, the unity of all, that any ultimate meaning, understanding, reality exists.

Within the swirling cosmos of physical and spiritual existence, within the dimensions of our knowledge and within dimensions beyond our knowing and owning, within symbols and formulae and concepts already understood and ways of expression not yet even dreamt of, within the bounds of that which exceeds all bounds we dare describe, are an infinitude of splinters, all revealing the whole, but none of them large enough to contain or be the whole.

To catch sight of the whole, we would need to have all the splinters, all the pieces and that which holds them all together — an infinite challenge.

Or

we would need to return to the vision of Blake, of seeing the all-that-is hinted at in any and all fragments of the whole — (an inviting prospect);

BUT, not mistake the fragments for the whole!

- - - -

When we resort to "sliver thinking" we do mistake the fragments for the whole.

We forget the essential unity of all-that-is, and we forget our participation in that same all-that-is.

All-that-is cannot exist without us in it. We cannot exist separate from all-that-is.

There is that essential unity.

All-that-is can never be separate from anything. Nothing can exist separate from all-that-is.

When we embrace that essential unity we see the slivers, the fragments for what they are, distinctive pieces of reality, but also only partial pieces of that larger unity.

Let me suggest an illustration.

The country of Italy is not the United States. I can look at Italy and see the Italian people, Italian culture, Italian architecture, Italian music, Italian foods, and Italian ideas. I can look at the United States and see her people, culture, architecture, music, foods, and ideas that are specifically U.S.

I can differentiate the two countries in many ways, and attribute to each its own identity.

I can see each for what it is.

But, if I stop there, and think the differentiations are the whole, I am looking only at fragments, at mere slivers.

And if I then look at all the countries in this way, I am making a world of fragments, but still ignoring the larger whole.

Being open, I want to see the whole picture, and not just that with which I am already familiar. In fact, it is my openness that has allowed me to even think about those things that seem other than me. Moving from a closed self-centeredness (another definition of openness would be a growing absence of self-centeredness), you can see beyond your own circle with both interest and clarity.

Connecting, I look for the ways that the fragments share similar traits, similar patterns. Moving from differences to commonalities (another definition of connected thinking would be the growing presence of relatedness), you can see beyond your own circle of experience to a larger world of shared meaning.

Thinking unity, I want to see the ways in which a greater whole is revealed in the web of connections that comprises the world I experience. Moving from fragments to a unified whole (another definition of unifying thinking would be the growing awareness of an essential reality that transcends anything specific), you can see beyond your own circle of specific connections to an all-encompassing unity that is all-that-is.

When one finds that sense of unity, no fragment stands alone, separate. True, some remain seemingly separate like those pieces of a jigsaw puzzle which don't seem to fit. "Are you sure these are from this puzzle?" you ask. But then, later, when some other pieces are in place, they suddenly fit.

Have you ever had that experience?

You experienced something or someone, and did not know where to place that experience in your sense of a larger picture?

It was hard to sense a unity that included that experience.

What was it for you?

For me, what comes to mind most forcefully are a number of life experiences that stretch back decades, small glimpses into a world of spiritual connection that made little sense at the time. In fact, they seemed quite outside the empirical, scientific world in which I was then centered. I would have these events, things like out-of-body awareness, past-life recognition, profound "peak experiences", and not know where to put them in my life understanding. I thought I knew the whole of my understanding, and these were outside that whole.

Then, in the aftermath of my daughter's death, in the months in which I could not mount any of my usual defenses, I began to first sense, then experience, then understand that what I had known was only a small fragment of a larger picture, and those pieces of experience I had previously thought not a part of that picture now fit very naturally into that emerging larger picture.

Have you found a way to fit those pieces that once seemed outside your world inside a wider world? What happened? What changed for and in you?

One of our human challenges is to realize that we cannot experience anything that is outside of our world of meaning. It may defy our present definition, but it cannot exclude itself from the larger whole which is the essential us within an essentially unified world.

Again, sliver thinking, seeing only the fragments, allows us to think things can happen to us that don't belong in our worlds of meaning.

I am reminded of so many of the world's great novels – be it *Les Misérables, Don Quixote, Great Expectations, Jane Eyre, The World According to Garp, The Color Purple* – in which we are invited into the life story of some person. Meals are eaten, trips taken, words exchanged, events observed, fears faced, loves won and lost. It is only

Reclaiming the Sould of Your Faith

in the last chapter, sometimes in a post-death epilogue, that we learn of the ways in which those meals, trips, words, events, fears, loves were woven in that life.

Had any of those central characters chosen only one set of slivers from the whole, how would their lives have been different?

Even we, reading of those lives, don't know what will be essential or important until the whole story is known, and then all the parts fit.

How about for yourself? Have you ever opted to focus only on one subset of your experiences? What happened?

Without the whole, not only is the whole lost, but then the significance of most of the fragments is also lost.

Since we don't know the unified whole, when we choose one sliver over the rest in the limitation of fragmented thinking and living, we are choosing blind. But if we are focusing on only one fragment, we cannot know the unified whole.

Is that the way you want to go?

It is the difference between sensing, seeing, living "this <u>or</u> that," or "this <u>and</u> that."

So, how do we know if we are thinking in a unitary way?

> Let me suggest a simple test (five easy questions).
> Do all the pieces of your life seem to fit meaningfully into your understanding of life?
> Do you find that your understanding of life has changed and expanded over the years?
> Do you welcome new experiences for the chance they bring to expand your sense of

understanding and meaning?

Do you have a sense that while you have integrated most of your experiences into your worldview, the reality of life is still larger than what you have already known?

Even in times of disillusion (when all the pieces don't appear to fit), do you still sense your participation in a larger unity?

If you can say "YES!" or even "I guess so," or even "I try to," to all five questions, then you are moving in or into unitary living.

If your answer wavers from the affirmative on any or all of them, you may still be focusing on the fragments rather than the unified whole. But, if that is the case, and you are still reading this, then you are open to moving in a new, renewing direction. Something here must be speaking to you, and now your task is to try to listen and discover what it is. Which of the questions is the one that spoke the most to you (and I do not mean which one caused you to say "No," but the one which most attracted your attention, your consideration, your time).

That is your opening edge. Follow that opening edge, and see where it takes you. You will be growing more into unitary thinking and living from that point.

The human condition is such that while many of us at given moments can say "YES" to those five questions, most of us at other time cannot do the same. The great, grand all-that-is unity in which we live and whose understanding we seek will always be with us and at the same time beyond us. We move into appreciation and understanding of it, and then some subsequent life experiences cause us to feel we don't have a grasp of it after all. We are one with it, and then it eludes us, and then we find it again.

Our challenge is not to think we can fully grasp the ultimate unity, but that we tend toward, move toward, desire toward, envision toward that unity.

This, then, is the third test of our faiths, as they are now,

and

this is the third criterion of the collective faith we wish to create and sustain:

Is this a model or mode that leads us to see a unified whole?

Are we being asked to understand in ways that are whole or fragmented?

Chapter 5
HOPEFUL
(Progressive)
FORWARD LOOKING vs. BACKWARD LOOKING

Let me make a bold assertion:
 There is nothing in nature which is inherently destructive.
Does this make sense to you?
If so, why, how?
If not, why not?

- - - -

Let me tell you why I make this assertion.

If we are open to the concept of the unity of all existence, then all that is within that existence must contribute to that existence. All the parts of the whole, without individual valuation or assessment, comprise the whole.

You and I do not know the whole; we only know some of the parts of that whole.

Yes, I will admit that we know parts of that whole which seem to be destructive.

What seemingly destructive parts come to your mind?
Why?

I know when I think of this, some events of my life leap out at me:

my dire encounter with cancer at the age of 25;

the fire that consumed half of my home when I was 32;
the birth and subsequent loss of my son, with grave medical problems, when I was 34;
a series of miscarried hopes for another child in the years that followed;
the dissolution of my marriage of 20 years;
my loss of a cherished position through the cancellation of the grant funding, with the subsequent upheaval of relocation;
the physical death of my daughter.

OK, Job, move over, I might say. (It is ironic that during the sabbatical in which I am writing this book I am living in the Parrochia of San Giobbe (St. Job) in Venice!)

This is a list of elements that could surely qualify to make the "Destructive Top Ten," if I wanted to see them in that way.

It is filled with fear, physical destruction, loss, daunted hope, and exile.

But, let me tell you about another life:

being a 40+ year cancer survivor when the 5-year rate was less than 50%;
always having a roof over my head, a bed beneath my body, and enough food to be sustained;
having the joy of having three wondrous daughters;
getting a second chance at marriage, and marrying my beloved Elissa;
learning through many losses to discover what really matters to me;
continuing to find meaningful expressions of my spirit

in my work;

being able to write about all of this and share it with you.

OK, Adam, move over, I might say.

This is a list of elements that could surely qualify to make the "Blessed Top Ten," if I wanted to see them in that way.

But, it is the same life.

The same events can be seen as destruction or blessings.

How about in your life?

Do you have your own set of "Destructive Top Ten" and "Blessed Top Ten"?

Which set of these do you use to describe your life?

Why?

- - - -

Think beyond any specific life to the world around all of us.

The essential seas which bathe the earth and made life possible are formed from the destruction of the isolation of hydrogen and oxygen, mated in the intense energy of their fusion.

The landmasses thrust up with volcanic violence, turning seas to steam.

The long rains upon the land, eroding the stone into soil from which land life could sustain itself.

The dead of each generation, enhanced by the soil from which it sprang, returning to that soil to enhance the soil.

The washing of the seas on shore to form sandy beaches.

The heat of the sun evaporating the waters of the earth.

The clouds of the heavens growing heavy with water until the rain falls.

Lightning strikes creating fires which consume the vegetation.

The burned vegetation returning its nurture into the chain of life.

New life, fueled by sun, soil, and water, grows upward, outward.

Nothing forming but what something else has dissolved.

An endless cycle of coming and going, each and every piece of it part of a larger whole.

A conscious spirit, gazing on it all from a great distance, would see none of the specifics, but only the pulsing of a small dot of a planet as the cycles of coming and going proceed.

An ever greater conscious spirit, gazing from an even greater distance, beyond the notions of time and space, would not even see the small dot, but only the almost breath-like rhythm of whole galaxies.

And encompassing all of that a still greater awareness, the awareness that is all-that-is, aware of itself, sensing the abiding presence of its total existence, the rhythmic manifestation of that existence, and the ever-growing realization of its potential.

How, then, can we, at our level of all of this, make any meaningful valuation or assessment of those parts without knowing the whole?

Yet, we do.

We judge some things to be good, and others to be bad,

as if we knew the whole picture. Beside misleading us in our assumption of our knowledge of the universal meaning of any given event, think about how this leads us down a road better left untaken.

In seeing things as good *or* bad, we resort to a dualism that we had hoped would be overcome with more unitary thinking and living. (Dualism is simply seeing anything as either this *or* that, without gradations of meaning or inclusion in some larger context of meaning.)

We also lead ourselves into the trap of good and evil, a trap which offers only disappointment or disillusionment at best without the intervention of some extraordinary force from outside the situation.

What do I mean by that?

Think again about my life as I shared it, or your own life as you remembered it.

If we were to choose the description of life only from the point of view of the negative elements and not see their participation in the whole, it would be very easy to be disappointed or disillusioned by the reality of the gift of this life. Each element would seem to take us further and further from the state of goodness which existed at some prior point in our life.

Once I was healthy, now I am less healthy.

Once I was married, now I am single.

Once I had a child, now I am alone.

Once I had a job that was fulfilling, now it is gone.

Once I _____, now I am _____.

Once, once, once ... but now ...

Do you get a sense of what is happening here.

Reclaiming the Sould of Your Faith

In isolating any event or series of life events from the unity in which it exists, we are thrown into looking back along the already familiar path of life. For most people, this look back brings with it a whole host of feelings: sadness, loss, regret, anger, guilt.

And a lack of empowerment - we only see those things that "happened" to us.

Such a litany of life is discouraging, robbing us of spiritual energy.

Have you ever felt that, like life was robbing you of your spiritual energy?

Underlying such a life-view, with that loss of spiritual energy, is a feeling that there is little we can do about it all. It seems hopeless.

It seems like there was a time, once, when things were better, but now it is all downhill. This echoes sentiments like "You are born, and it is one long downhill slide toward death."

But, remember now my bold assertion at the beginning of this chapter:

There is nothing in nature which is inherently destructive.

We already considered many of the forces of nature, from the primordial seas to the erupting volcanoes, from the erosion into the smallest grain of sand and the assemblage of great masses into galaxies, and saw that no one element could be seen as inherently destructive once the specifics are given up, and a larger, more unitary consideration was made.

Why then assume that life is an exception to this given?

Randolph W.B. Becker

Why think of life as if it were a destructive element?

But, that is what the usual religious message is.

Think for yourself about what you were taught by your family, or your religious community, or your culture.

Most people are taught that life is a great struggle against wandering away from some prior state of goodness, a losing struggle for most people, whose only hope (if there be any hope) is in the intervention of some force from outside of life. Life itself, in and of itself, does not have the inherent power to overcome the naturally destructive tendency of its own course. The unblemished slate at birth (or worse, the already blemished slate at birth) becomes more and more tarnished if one simply lives life.

Religions like these are trying to portray life as inherently destructive.

And most religions then add an additional element which is outside of life, some form of redeemer, savior, grace-giver, divine balancer, which becomes one's only hope.

Let's see if we have this all down:

> life is experienced as a series of destructive events, measured by a backwards glance to a time, in one's life or in the history of humanity, when things were better.
> since this is the nature of life, there is nothing that is natural that can overcome the process.
> our only hope is to have some super-natural force that can return us, if we are lucky or pious enough, into that once better state.

If all of this is truly so, then human life is not natural. It is somehow different from the rest of existence. But we know, if we are thinking unitarily, that human life cannot be separate from the rest of existence.

So, this *view* of life is what is unnatural, not life itself.

This *view* of life is what is destructive, not life itself.

And we know this, for any belief system which relies on something beyond the natural order of things for its hope, is hopeless.

Doesn't this make sense to you?

If I were to tell you that I was serving you chocolate cake, but then served you white cake and told you I had some chocolate syrup somewhere else, which I might or might not, depending on how you behaved, drizzle over your cake, would it, could it ever really be chocolate cake?

Looking backwards, seeing specifics as separate rather than as parts of a unity, understanding life as inherently destructive, with the only hope supernatural ... is that the cake you want served to you?

Then, what is the alternative?

We can look forward.

We can try to see events of our life in connection to a larger unity.

We can try to see the ways in which our lives and their events are building blocks.

And we can see that hope, like life, must be contained within all-that-is, and not separate from it.

All-that-is, which contains us all, also contains the future, all the events of our lives, all that we bring into being, and all hope. Nothing separate, nothing distant, nothing supernatural.

OK, you say, this is all well and good. But, what does this mean in my life?

Let's start with the notion of looking forward, for its contains all the other elements as well.

As we have already considered, looking backwards assumes that somewhere in the past, life and everything else was as it "should" be. If that is true, then the best that any life can do is to try to restore what has been. Nothing positive, just making up for the negatives.

But, if we are looking forward, then we have a belief that the future has the potential to be better than the past. There is still much to be brought into being, to be added to the total of all-that-is. The least we can do is to enhance what already has been. Everything can be positive, in the long run, building on what has already been.

Underlying this approach to life is a belief that everything that enhances life, everything that expresses it more fully, adds to the sum total of good. The basic unit that is all-that-is is the ultimate depository of all and that unit can be enhanced in its overall good. This builds on the this *and* that notion: that what we can do with our lives can add to the sum total of what exists. It is not simply offset by some other negative force (that would be some more of the dualistic thinking, that every yin must have its yang) but can be a positive enhancement to the unity of the whole.

In other words, in the future, all-that-is can contain more good than it does now. It's potential for goodness can be fulfilled. If, indeed, there is nothing in nature which is inherently destructive, then the playing field of life is at least level, neutral; we can make a difference.

So, in looking to the future, our role becomes less of memory, and more of vision. (Looking backwards is a task of memory ... trying to recall what has already been.)

But, what is vision?

It is the specific embracing of the ideal of unity in a proposed reality.

Huh?

It is specific – nothing vague here. Vision speaks about definite things to do, to think, to consider, to explore.

It embraces – this is not abstract, but almost physical. We are not just talking about things at a distance.

It is about the ideal of unity – our sense of unity which grew out of our openness and our realization of connection is made the focus of our living. We find ourselves again and again drawn to the larger unity rather than the smaller specifics.

It is about a proposed reality – how life might be if the values we claim to hold as dearest were to become the ordinary conditions of life. What we say is important to us would become the cornerstone of all that is, trying to express the greater all-that-is.

We are talking about doing specific things in a passionate way to try to make what we sense as ideal become reality.

We are talking about using our lives in constructive, forward-looking ways to make real what we hold in our hearts and minds and spirits as hope. Hope, not as a specific outcome, but as the belief that on the other side of any life event, there can be both meaning and in fact more meaning. Hope as an understanding that we can never become separated from the possibility of a greater understanding of life and all-that-is, except by our own failure to see the larger picture.

Looking forward says that we have not seen everything yet. And if there is nothing in nature which is inherently destructive, then what we have not yet seen can be wonderful, wondrous, worthy, welcomed.

This is the progressive concept ... that the flow of life forward brings us to new heights of our humanity. The larger unity in which we live can become enhanced as we help bring about a larger fulfillment of its potential.

But, let's get very specific.

What do you value? I mean really value. What aspects of life are so important to you that without them life would not be life?

What in your present life enhances those valued things?

What, in the future, could continue to enhance them, or enhance them more?

What would happen if those valued things were to be stripped away and all you could see were the values, not the things?

What then, are your values?

What could you do, with your life, to enhance, express, extend, embrace, encourage, emulate, energize those values?

If you did that, what could happen?

That is your hope!

I know that I value the potential of human beings as spiritual beings to be able to envision a world in which their values can be fulfilled. If you told me I am only physical, I would feel like I had just lost the core of life itself. So, I try to find those means by which I can be in touch with my spiritual being, and the spiritual being of others. But, if I and all of those others were to be stripped away, the spiritual potential in the universe would still be there – it is not contained in any specific physical being (not absent from any either). Therefore, I value our spiritual potential. And in this life I can focus on my own spiritual potential, and the spiritual potential of others in every way that I can. This book is just one of those expressions. My deep passion about that potential is another. My enthusiastic exploration of the spiritual understandings of others is another. And if all of the ways in which I use my life to value the spiritual potential that exists, then the world of spirit and the world of matter would no longer be seen as separate, but as the whole that I know it to be. And just thinking about that, sensing that I have progressed to the point that I can see such a future, gives me so much hope I cannot measure it.

This is my pattern of values and hope.

What is your pattern of values?

How could you shape your life so those values were enhanced by the very fact of your existence?

How would that shape the future you envision?

Does that give you hope?

- - - -

This, then, is the fourth test of our faiths, as they are now,

and

this is the fourth criterion of the collective faith we

wish to create and sustain:

Is this a model or mode that leads us to look at life with a very natural, empowering hope?

Are we being asked to understand in ways that are forward looking or backwards looking?

Chapter 6
FREEING
LIBERATING vs. CONFINING

Do you remember when you were younger, and you would start the school year with a set of new clothes? Your parent would help you decide on sizes, and often tried to talk you into something with a little "growing room." But you insisted on things that would look just right the first day of school.

Some nine or ten months later, if you could have been forced to wear those same clothes, you would have looked like you were prepared for floods, had grown monster arms, and taken on some unwanted poundage.

The same clothes that once upon a time fit perfectly, allowing you to move freely and comfortably, had become confining, restricting your ease of movement.

You grew, and they did not.

Well, faith can be like clothes ... fitting perfectly, allowing freedom and comfort of movement, or ill-fitting, confining a person to a limited range of thoughts, emotions, and beliefs.

Have you worn the same clothes all your life? Probably not.

Have you had the same faith all your life?

- - - -

If we turn to any of the world's scriptures, we will find stories of people who struggled with this very problem.

Do, I, asks Mohammed, continue to live as my

tribesmen have for generations, wearing the same spiritual clothing? Or do I dare think of a new way of being?

Do I, asks Jesus, continue to live out the rules of my Judaism, staying within the tradition? Or do I dare think outside the laws of the Torah?

Do I, asks the Buddha, continue to live in princely splendor, enjoying the fruits of my heritage? Or do I dare live outside the palace, with the common people?

Spiritual traditions are founded on the willingness of courageous men and women to dare to feel free enough to move outside of the religious paths they have inherited. They liberate themselves from what has been, choosing a new path that leads forwards, not backwards.

Religions are founded by making suits of spiritual clothes out of the new fabric daringly woven by the spiritual pioneers.

This is important enough that I want to repeat it.

Spiritual traditions begin with the courageous choice by men and women to feel free enough to create a new fabric of faith.

Religions take that new fabric and make a one-size-fits-all suit of clothes from it, which you are asked to fit yourself into and wear no matter how poorly it may fit in the future.

Spiritual traditions begin being about change, about freedom, about liberation.

Religions end up being about continuity, confinement,

and restrictions.

Does this match your faith experience?

How have you experienced the difference between spirituality and religion?

And that begs the question, do you want a spiritual faith or a religious faith?

- - - -

How does this happen? How do the spiritual insights of a visionary become the religion requirements of an institution?

Most people do not trust themselves.

Do you trust yourself?

As I am aging, I find that I trust myself more than I did when I was younger. There was a time when I would sit quietly in the corner of any discussion and listen to see if there would be any room in the opinions of the others for my point of view. I would only offer my own insights if I had a sense that they would be welcomed. I did not trust what I saw, what I felt, what I believed enough to be willing to risk putting it out in public.

Have you ever checked out a group before speaking your heart's desire?

Why?

If you are like me, it was probably because most people do not like to feel alone. We are, as mentioned before, social beings. And if we have taken to heart the idea of connection, we want to facilitate connection rather than accentuate differences.

I did not want to stand out. I did not want to have to defend my beliefs. I did not want to have to risk.

Reclaiming the Sould of Your Faith

Sound familiar in your own life?

Now, think back to what it must have been like to one of the earliest followers of one of the spiritual visionaries. Picture, if you will, being an early follower of Jesus.

You may have been lucky enough to have heard him preach several times. Maybe you even got to one of the post-gathering dinners. This man and his message ignited something in your spirit. Then, in a flurry of activity, covered over by a staged trial and execution, he seemingly was gone. But then he re-appeared, and then he was gone again.

"Is this really happening to me?" could have been a pretty normal response.

You continue to have the spiritual insights that this man gave you, but now he has gone somewhere. When you listen to those around you, you hear great amounts of fear in other people's words in relation to this man.

Dare you speak what is your heart's desire?

Dare you risk being open?

Do you trust yourself enough to do that?

And most people, in such times of transition and fear, do not trust themselves enough. It would feel too lonely to do so.

But then, suddenly, a chance.

In a conversation with another, you hear speak words you had heard Jesus say to you. She tells you about a group of people who have shared your experience. Do you want to join them in a discussion? There is even a local Jewish gathering at which some of his sermons are being re-preached as the sabbath services. Do you want to join in?

And you, a little afraid and more than a little excited, say "Yes!"

So you find yourself in a small gathering of about 20 people who have been keeping a deep spiritual secret, but who now feel they can share. So, one after another speaks some of the truths that you have heard and embraced. How exciting! How affirming!

But wait!

Now someone is telling of some event you attended, but interpreting it differently. There is a rush of conversation.

And finally you startle yourself by saying, "Look, if we are going to have any strength as his followers, we better get our own story straight!"

And at that point, a spiritual tradition becomes a religious tradition.

A person trading his or her own lack of trust in self for the protection and security of a shared faith system.

No longer would a sentence have to begin, "I believe," but rather, "We believe."

And in exchange for that security, each person gives up some of her or his freedom.

I went through that phase as well, deciding that if I could not tell my whole faith pattern to others, then I would seek out a group in which the compromises would not be too great, and just settle for the security of the group.

Have you ever done that? Given up some of your freedom of thought and belief in exchange for feeling connected, secure, understood?

But the first ones to join in that meeting of 20 or so were the lucky ones. They got to work out the compromises by which the religion would embody their individual faiths. It was their choice to forsake some things in order to have the confidence of the group.

What about the next 10 who joined the discussion? Things were still somewhat fluid, changeable.

And the next 10 after that? And then the next 100?

Eventually, the institution of the religion became a test of entry rather than an invitation to shape the evolution of the institution.

In the evolution from spiritual tradition to religious tradition, rules get laid down which will not change for the future of that religious tradition.

This is as true of liberal religious traditions as it is of fundamentalist religious traditions. There is not a religious tradition without that hallmark feature, because without such it would not be a religious tradition.

And there are more identifying traits that separate spiritual and religious traditions.

Earlier I asked you to think of spiritual traditions being founded on courageous acts and beliefs outside of established patterns and religious traditions as being founded on the translation of those actions and beliefs into newly established patterns. One is liberating, the other confining.

Now I am asking you to think about spiritual traditions having many points of entry. You are free to come onto the pathway from many directions, in many ways. Religious traditions have limited, often only one, point of entry. You are confined to a single door.

Has that been your experience?

As I grew older, I found myself being more open with others about what I believed. Why? Probably because I found that the safety and security I had sought through compromises eventually robbed me of my own special voice.

Even the most inclusive compromise will still ask you to give up something. Even the most inclusive religious tradition is exclusive in some way.

And often I found that what I was being asked to give up was the very thing that mattered most, the growing edge of my faith. Where the familiar meets the horizon, out beyond where the group has been willing to explore as a community, where I find the breezes of freedom of thought and expression ... that's where I find those things which the compromised group does not want to include.

But they are too important to me to keep in silence.

Age has its benefits – one learns that the worst someone else can do with an idea that shocks them is to be shocked. And that does not have to do with me!!

I finally learned that reactions to my beliefs are not about me, but about them.

I was selling my soul, so to speak, to feel comfortable, when in fact it was not my comfort I was protecting, but someone else's.

Ever done that yourself?

Thought you would not speak, thinking of how uncomfortable the reaction might feel, when in fact the reaction would be the sign of the other's person discomfort?

So now, I try to share what is my spiritual path.
I risk opening up.
Why?
Do I trust myself more? Probably.
But more than that, I have finally come to trust my faith more.
A faith that requires agreement, a faith that requires the assent of a community, a faith that can submit itself to compromise ... what kind of faith is that?

Spiritual traditions do not require agreement nor the assent of the community. They do not lend themselves to compromise. The flourish on their integrity.
Religious traditions begin in agreement, assent, and compromise. The flourish on integration.

So, another difference between the two.
Spiritual traditions welcome your faith as it is; religious traditions ask you to temper your faith to their parameters.
Have you experienced that?
If so, how? How did that feel?

There are still stages ahead for me in this life. One of the ones that most intrigues me is the role of the elder. These are women and men who have arrived at a place in this life journey at which they can begin to reflect back on what they have experience, who they were and who they have become. They can try to express those things that they have learned and remembered along the way.

Most of these people have already been declared obsolete by the institutions of their lives – executives, judges, chefs, professors, ministers, rabbis, imams, nurses, directors, mothers, father who have been "retired" because of their age. At least that is the explanation we are asked to accept.

But when I talk to these people, I find few of them have "retired", and most of them have advanced. They reach a point in life where they are no longer willing to just say what is expected of them by reason of institutional agreement, assent, or compromise. They often leave the "work force" because they no longer want to deal with concepts like 9-5, Human Resource Department forms, corporate policy, congregational boards, etc. They have a sense of what is really important to them.

And they do not hesitate to share what is important to them.

They speak out about their faith.

It is almost like they finally rip off a suit of ill-fitting institutional uniform clothing and stand naked before the world and say, "Hey, like it or not, this is me!"

I have spoken with many of them, and one word that comes up over and over again is "free." They feel a freedom in life even within the limitations of physical decline and even financial decline.

(Now, I will be quick to add that not everyone who reaches an advanced age feels this way ... and that is more of a challenge to me than a contradiction of what I am saying. And from these more timid people I hear more and more about their choice of maintaining connection to

Reclaiming the Sould of Your Faith

institutions as opposed to expressing their own faith.)

That freedom is often expressed as a sharing of a faith that sounds like Swiss cheese. It starts out looking like a whole block of faith, but when you slice into this way and that way, you see the large holes, which are questions, unanswered, unresolved questions. In fact, just like Swiss cheese, their faith would not be the real thing without the holes.

And how do they feel about this?

As one man in his mid-90's said to me, "There is nothing more freeing than to admit you don't have the answer to everything, and that in fact no one does."

In my next chapter, I will explore this concept in more depth, because I have found that for people with a vital faith a sense of eternal questioning is imperative.

For now, let's just remember one more difference between spiritual traditions and religious traditions.

Spiritual traditions offer the freedom of not having to explain everything while religious traditions suppose an explanation to everything, even if they do not have a convincing answer for certain things. One liberates a person to be with the emerging unknowns while the other confines one to the knowns.

Is this consistent with your experience?

Picture, if you will, a large train terminal. It is a Terminal, one at which the tracks come to a stub end, not a Station, in which the tracks only pass through. You are standing in the main hall, and you look up to the announcement board. There are many trains arriving.

Randolph W.B. Becker

Most from the same origin, most marked as "Limited." On the departure board, there is listed only one departure, to one place, and that one has the note "Reservations Required, Supplement Payable."

Then picture you are at a Union Station, where the tracks of many different railroads pass through. You look up at the announcement board, and find there are many trains arriving, from lots of different places, some on time, some early, some late. You also see that there are many, many trains leaving as well, some for the main line, some for scenic branch lines, some marked "Special", and at the bottom the sign says "all trains unreserved."

Which place would you like to be in?

Where would you feel freer?

Why?

Spiritual traditions are more like the stations, points of connection for many different lines of travel. Non-linear, web-like constructs of paths, which happen to converge at this time and this place. At that time and place, you may have come from almost anywhere, and you are free to choose to go wherever you want to go. There are no special requirements to hop aboard.

Religious traditions are more like the terminals, points of arrival from which there is only one advertised departure, reserved for only some. A very linear, single-track construct of one "true way" which leads those lucky enough to this time and place, from which you have little or no freedom as to where you can go next.

This final difference talks about options as opposed to tracks. It is not a dualistic model, however, because even through the station run tracks. The station gives you tracks and choices; the terminal just gives you a track. One liberates while the other confines.

When I reach the final stop on this earthly journey, this time around, I am hoping that I will find it is a station, and not a terminal. But isn't that the word we use so often about life? Terminal. Even that terminology is confining. I have come so far from my youth, when I would keep my faith quiet inside myself for lack of trust of self, I hope that at that final station I will not only feel liberated, but act liberated, and feel free to choose whichever track I want without worrying about how I will fit into it, or it will fit onto me. And I surely do not want to get on that next train wearing the clothes I wore to the first day of Kindergarten.

- - - -

In thinking about spiritual versus religious traditions, we noted this comparison:

SPIRITUAL:	RELIGIOUS:
free-form	rules
many points of entry	single point of entry
integrity (no compromise)	integration (assent, agreement, compromise)
unknowns (questions)	givens (answers)
many paths, non-linear	one path, linear

Now, if you are like I am, you will scan this chart and note the comparisons, left to right, right to left.

But I invite you to do something different. Take a piece of heavy paper (good use for some of that junk mail you get) and cover one of the columns, so you only those things which are labeled SPIRITUAL or RELIGIOUS.

Stay with one column for a period of time, and read down the list of qualities. What feelings do these qualities evoke in you? Why?

Then, switch to the other column, and ask the same question about feelings.

What were your feelings? Did one column appeal more to you than the other? Why?

If your openness, sense of connection, sense of unity, and hopefulness have brought you to this place, are you able to appreciate what a liberation of your spirituality from the confines of religion might mean?

Is this familiar ground, or is this your cutting edge of faith?

- - - -

This, then, is the fifth test of our faiths, as they are now,

and

this is the fifth criterion of the collective faith we wish to create and sustain:

Is this a model or mode that leads us toward freedom of faith?

Are we being asked to understand in ways that are liberating or confining?

Reclaiming the Sould of Your Faith

A short post-script to this chapter. Am I, some might ask, suggesting that everyone who gets to this point will want to leave their religious traditions and communities?
No!
Quite the contrary. They will probably want to stay and see if those traditions can grow as much as they have. Or, if they cannot grow that way, can a new expression be created to include valued tradition <u>and</u> the newly embraced freeing faith.

Remember, all of those great leaders we talked about in the beginning of this chapter tried to incorporate their newly found sense of freeing faith into their traditions. Only their followers felt the need to leave those traditions and establish themselves separately. In other words, if you find a freeing spiritual tradition inside yourself, you will probably not need to leave your religious tradition. If you want to found some new religious tradition that will make rules out of the new freedom you have found, then you will have to leave. But, then you will have chosen to exchange one religious tradition for another, not simply follow the liberating spiritual message you are discovering.

Chapter 7
CONTEMPLATIVE
QUESTIONS vs. ANSWERS

If you took Geometry as I did in high school, you experienced a very contemplative activity. Beginning with a point !, you then connected two points! _____ ! with a line. From there angles, line segments, arcs, bisected lines, and all the rest flowed. Each proof you rendered not only became the basis of future understandings and proofs, but each proof raised its only questions. In geometry, you never come to an ending, wherein all the proofs are known, and all of physical space proven.

The recent discussion within physics about a unified theory to accurately describe physical reality now proposes that only at ten dimensions do we get an adequate description. The geometry we studied had two, or maybe for a few of us, three dimensions. Yet, none of the ten dimensions can begin to be described without the geometry of those two or three we studied. And if today the number is ten, what will the number be in the future?

This is contemplative activity because:

an answer to one question becomes the basis for further answers,

an answer to one question poses at least one, and often more new questions,

there is no ultimate point at which all answers will be known.

A contemplative activity is one in which the infinite is

embraced by seeing itself as a single element in a never-ending process of understanding.

And contemplative activity is not limited to the physical world.

My wife and our three daughters provide me with ample evidence. Just when I think I have understood the totality of my love for them, I discover a new level of that connection. Even as my love, my feeling of connection, awakens more of me, building as it does upon what has been, I sense that there are dimensions to our relationships which are yet to be.

Have you experienced this?

To me, this is a direct result of living life freely, of seeing my life experiences as liberating rather than confining. If I believe that there are no ultimate walls, no profound boundaries to limit such vitals of existence as hope, love, and spirit, then I also see that there can be no walls or boundaries formed by answers. Answers become doorways, not barriers.

But, if you are like many people, you learned about religion in a question and answer format in which the central questions were posed by the religion, and the answers were also posed by the religion.

Does this ring a bell?

In fact, most religious traditions are founded on a very definite set of questions and answers. Some traditions look to written scripture, and say forcefully, every question you can imagine has an answer in our ancient words.

Some traditions look to wise leaders of the past, and

say forcefully, every question you can imagine has already been answered by our ancient teachers.

Some traditions look to ceremonial leaders of the present, and say forcefully, every question you can imagine either has been or can be answered by our divine leader.

Some traditions look to ritualized actions, and say forcefully, every question you can imagine can be answered by participating in our rituals.

Does one of these answers describe religion's approach to life's questions as you have experienced it?

What do you see as common in each of these models?

I see religions again being
exclusive,
> *We have **the** answers,*
differentiating,
> *unlike others.*
fragmented,
> *Our answers are the best out of all the options,*
backward looking,
> *because we have historic precedent to show that.*
confining.
> *To be religious, you have to learn to live with our*
answers.

This is very much like taking a tour of a foreign city. You are on the tour bus (or boat) and the guide tells you that you have chosen the best tour company in town. In fact, the part of the city you will see is the only really important part. You are instructed to look to your left to see this or that. You ask about what is on the right, and are told that there is nothing there to ask about, nothing of meaning. But you insist in your asking about the right side of the street. You are told that the important sights are all on the left. You ask on what basis the guide says this, since you just saw something very interesting out of the right side. And the guide says because the time-honored script says so, and in doing this for twenty years this has been true, and that no one before has ever questioned this. And then the guide adds that if you want to get the most out of the tour, you should only pay attention to the tour as it is being presented. And please hold all questions until the end of the tour, when you can get your own copy of the tour script which will answer all questions.

If you were on such a tour, what would you do?
Feel you had that coming?
Apologize, and focus to your left, as instructed?
Sit there and fume?
Continue to ask questions? (Even though that might get you hard stares from others)
Press the issue of how the tour was organized? (and risk being kicked off)
At the next stop, ask to get off?
Go back and explore the same streets through your own eyes?
Tour on your own, where you want to go, where your questions take you?

Do you recognize yourself in any of these reactions to such a tour?
Let's look at it again, in another way,

If you were on such a tour, what would you experience/express:

> *Self-blame* - Feel you had that coming?
>
> *Fear* - Apologize, and focus to your left, as instructed?
>
> *Anger* - Sit there and fume?
>
> *Aggression* - Continue to ask questions? (Even though that might get you hard stares from others)
>
> *Confrontation* - Press the issue of how the tour was organized? (and risk being kicked off)
>
> *Assertiveness* - At the next stop, ask to get off?
>
> *Self-control* - Go back and explore the same streets through your own eyes?
>
> *Contemplation* - Tour on your own, where you want to go, where your questions take you?

Now, do you still see yourself in the same reaction?

If yes, does the added description remind you of what you often experience or express?

If no, why do you see yourself differently now? Was it that the added description did not fit you, or that you don't like/want that description to fit you?

I want to introduce you to eight people I have known in my thirty years in ministry. Listen to their stories, and sense if you see yourself in any (or all) of them, some maybe from your past, maybe some from your present, and hopefully some from your future.

I met Rose when she was in her early sixties. She told me she had grown up in a very religious household. They had observed every holiday, every ritual, every letter of the "divine" law. She had attended religious schools, being a straight A student. She remembers being in fourth grade and asking about how God could be everywhere and only be in their religion. As she told me this story, she said very quickly and quietly, "I know I shouldn't have asked that, but I did." She continued her story, of her separation from her family in her thirties, her journey through a non-religious phase, and then finally her recent membership in the congregation I was serving. I asked her about how she was feeling about her life now, and her relationship with her family (once more reconnected now she was at least a member of "some religion"). She spoke of many conflicts in her feelings and her actions, and then posed some major questions about her newly chosen faith institution, but she prefaced it with, "I am sorry, I know it's my fault for having so many questions, and I shouldn't be asking this ..."

Self-blame

I met the man (I do not remember his name now) when I was serving as chaplain to one of the Mayo Clinic hospitals in Rochester, Minnesota. I was assigned to a ward to minister to those patients who did not have a local congregation (which was true of most of the people who came for many miles to be treated at Mayo) and were not either Roman Catholic, Jewish, or Lutheran (all having their own denominational chaplains). I came upon this eighty year old in his room late one afternoon. A quick look at his chart (we were considered staff at the same level as the physicians) told me he was there for more in-

Randolph W.B. Becker

depth exploration to see if there were any hopeful possibilities in his battle with cancer. I introduced myself, and asked if he would like me to sit down and talk for a while. The talk (by his direction, not mine) moved almost immediately to his religious life. He wanted to tell me about how he had been a member of the same church for nearly 65 years, having been baptized there as an infant and choosing membership when he was confirmed. He spoke forcefully about worshiping, studying, praying to make sure he got his faith right. He had a nearly perfect attendance record on Sunday mornings, and said he tried to not only understand what the minister would say, but try to turn it into action. He told me "I try to do exactly what I am told." I asked him, "Why?" Suddenly the rapid-fire recitation he had been making stopped. A long silence. Then, a weak, wavering voice answered, "Because I was afraid if I did not ..." and he could not continue. Another long silence. "If I did not, I would die ..." Another long silence. "I would die and go to hell."

Fear

Bill was a member of a congregation I served about twenty years ago. I could always count on Bill when I made my annual request for sermon topics for the coming year. Not only did he always suggest at least one topic, and often many more, in essence he suggested the same topic, over and over again. It was always some variant on the theme "Why _____ is wrong!!!!" He had a long list of those institutions and people who were wrong. Just giving the list was not enough. He wanted to have the whole congregation fume with him, joining him in his opinions.

One year I decided I would preach on one of his suggestions, and crafted what I considered a good sermon. I explored the intended institution of focus from an historical and a contemporary understanding, asking key questions about the integrity of its positions. I presented an analysis of the ways in which this institution was making choices in our own lives without our knowledge or consent, and suggested a series of five change actions that those equally concerned might adopt. He hated the sermon, and added me to his list, wanting everyone to know "Why Randy is wrong!" After about two weeks of this, I decided to confront him directly, asking him what had I done that was wrong. He fumed about inconsequentials for a few minutes (wrong songs chosen for the service, did not like the readings I had chosen) but then raise his voice in volume and pitch a full notch:

"You had no right to let them off the hook so easily by implying that we could do some simple things to change the way it is. I don't want them understood and changed. I want them to suffer just like they have made me and many others suffer. I'm not going to put any of my energy into that crap you suggested, and I sure am not going to put myself out there on the line so they can get at me again."

Anger

Anita was not a member of the congregation I was serving in New England, but she liked to attend our events and worship. She said that she did not want to join because of the way that the religion of her childhood had treated her so badly. However, her attendance was often more like a drive-by shooting than participation. Her pattern was always to arrive late, after the introduction, yet she would want to sit in the front row, either moving to an empty chair or dragging a chair up front. If there was a time for some special sharing in the course of the meeting or worship, she always had something to share, and share at length. If there were a time for questions and answers, she would have many questions, and she would insist that all of her questions be dealt with when it was her turn. And if she did not like the answers she would be given, by myself or the group, she would re-ask the question. When I would ask her what she thought, she would snap back "What I think is not the question here. I want to have an answer to my question." Soon her arrival in a meeting or worship would be greeted by a noticeable knowing look from some in the congregation to others. When sharing time would come and she would stand to speak, one could almost hear a congregational sigh arise. When some of her friends spoke to her about her behavior, she cut them off with a quick "Well, I have the right to speak, don't I? No religion is going to keep me quiet!"

Aggression

For fifteen years, I was the director of a one-week summer camp for young people (from second grade through high school). In a community of about 100 children and youth, coupled with 25 staff, over the years we developed a tradition of activities, rules, expectations, and policies to ensure both the safety of our campers and fulfillment of our programmatic goals. For the most part we were a community of happy campers. But, two people come out of my memories when thinking about this topic.

One was an older teen, in his last year at camp, who began to act out a number of near-prohibited acts. As the week progressed, he pushed the limits with more and more force and more and more finesse. And each time I would talk to him, his refrain was the same "And who said it should be this way?" I always spoke about how we had generated these rules as a community, and that I was simply making sure they were observed. On the last night he finally pushed the limit too far, and in front of the whole community I had to tell him to stop. He turned on me, took a challenging stance, and said "And who made that rule? And who is going to enforce it? And what is going to happen?" As calmly as I could I said, "In this case, I made that rule, because you are being disruptive and not setting a good example. And I will enforce it if I have to. And that would mean that if you continue, I will ask you to leave camp." His reply was to yell "FACIST" at me and stomp loudly from the hall.

The other person was one of our staff. She could not manage to live by the rules either. She would smoke in front of the campers, she would not show up for her assignments on time, and she twice left the camp area without our knowledge. I confronted her on each of these issues, and her response was a routine "Yes, so what?" I would explain our policies and the basis for these (healthy examples, consistency in the behavior expected of campers and staff, etc.). "Yeah, yeah, sure," was always her response.

But her behavior continued. Finally I told her that she had a choice, either observe our rules or leave. Her response? "Hey, that's not being very liberal or religious.

You're not letting me follow my own beliefs. Who do you think you are, my father? And besides, who would you get to do my job ... so I guess you just got to live with it."

I spent the rest of the week covering her responsibilities as well as my own, after I asked her to leave.

Confrontation

Peter was a member of the Finance Committee for the cluster of congregations I served for many years. He was in the middle of his first three-year term when I arrived. When I attended the meetings, I was taken by Peter's manner in the meetings. In most instances, he would disagree with the majority opinion on matters as diverse as use of reserves, grant funding, risk-management, and social activism through investments. His disagreement always came as a well-researched and calmly presented statement, followed inevitably by a vote that would be 5-2 or 6-1. In over those two years, I can only remember one vote that went his way. But I remember at least 30 issues on which he spoke, knowledgeably and forcefully. I never heard him turn angry or confrontational. When his first term was just about up, he was asked to serve another term. He declined. When I asked him why, he said, "This is just not my way of doing things. I've tried to advocate the best I could, but I think it is time to move on."

Assertiveness

I met Penny in a community based adult learning program where I was teaching a class about theology. Penny was brought up in a fundamentalist religious community, one with very definite answers to a very limited set of questions. Even through her teen years, she did not challenge the strict social rules. She married within the community, and soon was the mother of two children. Her husband farmed, she baked and cooked, and the family was religious together. She and her husband, in the profound intimacy of their marriage, found a new freedom to talk about things which had been unspoken of before. She and he had questions beyond the set of acceptable questions, and questions about the definite answers they had learned. They each found that rather than avert their eyes from the world around them, they liked to look at what could be seen. Each new glimpse brought more questions, questions un-imagined in the closed community of their upbringing. She told me that these questions did not bother her, but her husband's reactions to them did. At first, he seemed afraid of them, speaking of them only with the lights out, in the safety of their bed, with the covers pulled way up. But, over a period of about three years, she detected a shift, as he began to not only speak of these things with her, but with others, more and more often with a twinge of anger in his voice. On one sabbath, he had arisen in the community worship and asked a question about the society outside. The elders at first stayed silent, but his insistence caused them to ask for his silence. That was the day he left, left them, left her.

Not long after that she too had left, not so much in anger as in sadness. She said she also felt a strange measure of hope, that she might be about to see the world through her own eyes for the first time. She told me she was in my class to have a context in which to go back and revisit all the questions and answers she had known for most of her life. She told me she was finding a peace with her own life, on her own terms, in her own way.

Self-control

I become much more personal with my last memory. I think of my grandfather on my mother's side. In his life he had gone from being a farm boy riding his horse several miles each day to get to school, to being a graduate of Colgate by the time he was 20, to having a Master's degree from Columbia, studying with John Dewey. He taught high school sciences, wrote many of the nationally-used workbooks in those subjects, became a high school principal, was honored with a Doctorate from Columbia, and eventually was Superintendent of Schools. After retirement he went on to a second career in human resources with an insurance company, and when their mandatory retirement age of 80 was reached, he began a third career with the employee credit union. Well into his 90's when he left the credit union, his mind never retired.

He had joined the rural Christian Church when he was 15, and took to heart the pledge of clean living he made at that time. He did not smoke, drink, curse; the Mosaic Ten Commandments were never tarnished by his life. But I never heard him preach about it. Indeed, I never heard him provide a dogmatic answer. He was too filled with questions. He once told me, "you can never know enough to not have more questions." Toward the end of his life, he and I talked several times about his thoughts of what lay ahead. He spoke in terms of a seemingly traditional view of God and heaven. But then he added, "But I know I will some more questions about it all when I get there." In the face of the "ultimate" life answer, he would still have questions!

Contemplation
Which of these people do you identify with?
Before? Now? In the future?
Why?
Do you sense the way in which the energy focus shifted in these stories?

For the first people, the answers controlled their energy. The answers created blame, fear, anger. The people were not in control.

For the next set of people, the answers also controlled them, by attracting their energy. Aggression, confrontation, assertiveness – all expressed over-and-against those answers. The answer continued to demand their attention, even while the people were increasingly setting their own emotional agenda.

In the last set of people, the energy was flowing to their questions. Self-control and contemplation imply an intentionality about the use of energy in the process of freely exploring life.

And how would you like your energy to be used?
In reaction or response to the answers of others, or in the construction of your own questions?

Any specific answers, as we talked about in the beginning of this chapter, belong to a faith world we would like to leave behind.

Randolph W.B. Becker

As open, connected, unitary, hopeful, and free as we might want to be, as long as we allow the answers of others to shape or attract our energies, we cannot gain, or regain, our own faith. Only as we move to be contemplative, to truly honor our own life questions by making them a worthy focus of our energies, will we fully embrace the other qualities we say we would like to honor.

This, then, is the sixth test of our faiths, as they are now,
>**and**

this is the sixth criterion of the collective faith we wish to create and sustain:

Is this a model or mode that leads us toward a contemplative life?

Are we being asked to understand life in terms of questions or answers?

Chapter 8
INDEPENDENT INFLUENCES INSTITUTIONS vs. BEING INFLUENCED BY INSTITUTIONS OF CULTURE

For several years I have been fortunate to be asked to serve on the allocations panel of my local United Way. Our task is to evaluate the various member agencies and their requests for funding in order to best allocate the always-less-than-requested available funds. Each year three agencies would be assigned to the sub-panel on which I sat along with about 4 others from the community. In a series of three meetings with each agency, we would get an in-depth view of the agency's goals, programs, methodologies, management, and finances.

I was surprised in the first two years of this work how often I heard the phrase "locus of control."

Do you know what this means?

It is a social psychological term that refers to the image a person has of her or his relationship to the social and physical environment.

For example, the old Flip Wilson line, "The Devil made me do it!" indicates a locus of control outside of the individual. It is a way of saying, "I had no choice. I was made to do it. I had no control. I was controlled."

Contrast that notion with the famous passage from Henry David Thoreau's *Life at Walden Pond*, "I went to the woods because I wish to live deliberately, to front only the essential facts of life." Here is a person wanting to express his own definition of his life. "I can be deliberate. I can choose. I have control."

Most of us would probably fall somewhere between these two loci, the two points of understanding.

When we encountered the term in the United Way work, it was because a variety of agencies had found that in their work with people of all ages, one of the best indicators of success was a person's sense that their locus of power was within themselves. Educational programs which helped people to explore and claim their own sense of self, without any other specific content area, were found to be more helpful dealing with problems of addiction and violence than were programs focused more narrowly on the addiction or the violent behavior itself.

When people could claim more of their lives as their own, they were less likely to allow outside influences to control them.

Does this make sense to you?

To me, this is a natural outgrowth of several values we have already considered: Freeing and Contemplative.

What could be more confining, more based solely on answers, than the notion that all the choices of life are outside of oneself?

What could be more freeing and contemplative than the notion that we are independent in our ability to make meaning and shape our response to life's events?

As you think about your own life, how do you see

yourself?

A maker of choices, or the recipient of choices made other than by yourself?

Again, probably most of us will fall somewhere between the consummate meaning-maker and the obedient pawn. Yet, along the line between the two poles, we probably tend toward one end or the other on this spectrum of independence.

How would you respond to these statements:

> I am usually the master of my own fate, the captain of my own ship.
> When things happen I do not like, I take it personally.
> I more regret not acting than the actions I have taken.
> Life has dealt me a bad hand.
> Others have more choices in their lives than I do.
> There are some things over which I am powerless.
> What happens to me in life is my own responsibility.
> People like me do not get a fair deal out of life.
> I can never hope to know what I should do.
> Life occurs according to laws which I did not make and cannot change.
> Some people are lucky, and some are not.
> I cannot choose what happens to me, but I can choose how I will react to it.
> There is a purpose to life, and so I need to go with the plan.

> I can make meaning in my life.
> This list is testing and measuring me.
> I am seeing myself through the eyes of these statements.

Now, if you are expecting that I will now reveal the key to these statements ("Give yourself a 1 if you said 'yes' to numbers 3, 5, 6, 9 ..."), you will be disappointed.

You need to "grade" your responses, but in terms of what they said to you.

Were there some which you found easy to answer "yes" or "no"?

Were there some which challenged you more, since no answer came easily?

Were there some which made you say "yes <u>and</u> no"?
Were there some that made you smile?
Were there some that made you angry?
Were these some that made you sad?

What do you find yourself saying to yourself after thinking about these statements?

Can you sense where you might fall on the line between seeing yourself in control and being controlled?

Let's go back and consider each of the statements, for they each and they all reveal some important concepts in a transition to more independence.

I am usually the master of my own fate, the captain of my own ship.

The independent person would probably be able to say

this without reservation. Yet, it is not implying the "rugged individualism" that might appear at first glance. This is an independence tempered by reality and interconnection.

It would be foolhardy to think that anyone would always have a sense of total control. A person with a high level of internalized control would need to be extremely honest (and hence realistic) with him/herself. Such honesty would lead a person to accept that we do not, as human beings at this point in our growth of perception and understanding, know everything. In fact, if someone were to tell you that they always felt and knew they were in control that might be a good indication of delusion!

Or not.

If fate is the overall outflowing of one's life and not the living out of some external script, then a very honest person could well declare that her or his "fate" was always internally script.

A key here is whether a person feels that fate describes a pattern that is unfolding or a pattern that is being created.

What do you think of when you read the word "fate"?

Maybe this analogy will help us. A merchant in Venice wants to ship goods to Norfolk. So, a ship is hired, appropriate to the cargo, and orders are given for delivery. The ship, under the direction of its captain, loads the cargo and sets sail. The captain is well aware that the journey cannot be made without the help of the crew and it will be constrained by the realities of straits, channels, winds, weather, and the physical curve of the earth. When the ship successfully unloads its cargo in Norfolk, having taken a certain route from Venice under the control of the captain, one could argue that the captain made the voyage happen. Yet, at the same time, the ship was not free to go wherever it wished, the captain could not have done it alone, the cargo would not have arrived without the appropriate ship. We know that other ships will not be as successful. We know that other ships may arrive even faster. Some captains will strain the crew to the point of mutiny while others will seem more like just a leading crewmember. No one thing fated the ship to complete the voyage as it did, but at the same time the captain, using the resources and opportunities available, shaped the voyage to its successful completion.

Now, if the cargo is your life, and the future is your destination, and you are the ship, how good a captain will you be?

Will you shrink from your duty?

Will you claim the dangers of the journey outweigh your abilities?

Will you become tyrannical in trying to control everything other than, or including yourself?

Or will you take charge, responding to the needs of the day in cooperation with other resources?

In other words, will you shape more than be shaped?
What do you do? Are you more the shaped or the shaper?

Randolph W.B. Becker

When things happen I do not like, I take it personally.

Shaping one's world is not the same as seeing oneself as the center of all creation. Yet, for almost all of us, our egos propel us toward this notion. In the prevalent dualism (the old "this or that" thinking), either something is about us or we don't matter at all. Our egos like to think that we matter to some degree, so we feel impelled to move ourselves toward an ultimate center stage.

Yet, this would imply that everything that happens is about us, personally. Let's consider how true and untrue this can be.

Someone who claims to love and care about you acts in some way that seems to you to be inconsiderate of your feelings. You take it personally. However, you cannot know in the absence of a discussion about it whether those actions were about you, or them, or something completely separate from either of you. For example, you are invited to dinner and discover that one of the dishes has been made with butter. You do not eat butter. It's not your thing. And they know that. Is this about you? Maybe. But maybe when they went to the market to get the oleomargarine, there was none, so the butter was the only option. Or maybe the recipe, already in preparation, had been very clear: do not use a substitute for the butter. See, it could have been circumstances, not you.

However, by taking it personally, you may not only skew the situation, you may also rob yourself of a chance to be expressive of your own values. When you focus on what "others" do that you perceive as being "done to you",

you use energy that could be used to shape your own response.

Which would be better in the example given, assume the intent being about you as you blame the other person, or take control of the situation and not eat the food.

When you make everything personal, you actually energize everything but yourself.

What do you feel – is your focus on what happens to you, or on what you can do about what happens?

I more regret not acting than the actions I have taken.

Ah, guilt.

Living a life of regret.

Do either of these options reflect a sense of expressing one's self?

Both are backward looking.

Both focus energy on things in the past, but with one difference.

When our focus is on what we have done, there is little we can do to undo that.

When our focus is on what we might do, there is still the potential to do it.

If all we do is rue what was or was not done, there is little difference.

But if we can learn from what we now (with hindsight) see we should have done, and we remember that point of learning as we proceed into the future, it can help us shape a future of which we can be proud.

Which do you look to in your past – what you did that you regret or what you have yet to do?

Life has dealt me a bad hand.

There is nothing more draining of the spirit, in my opinion, than the assumption of victimhood status.

I, like so many of us, can make a list of what has occurred in my life (as I did in Chapter 5). It can be easy, even tempting, to see life poured out as a series of bad things happening to us. We all seek answers to such questions as Rabbi Kushner posed in his popular book "When Bad Things Happen To Good People." If we have decided that most things that occur in life happen to us, then we see the locus of control for those events outside of ourselves. All those bad things are the work of *them*: others, family, neighbors, school, religion, government, society, life, God.

But has nothing good ever happened in your life?

Where did that good come from? If all that has been "bad" has been the work of *them*, then would it not follow that all the good also comes from *them*. That is where the assumption of victim status takes one. Out of the loop of life, into the status of mere pawn. One has bad days, one has good days, one has a bad life, one has a good life – it is all according to some external script. It is like someone else is the dealer, and the cards are stacked against you.

For a moment, let's follow that analogy. You sit down to a card game. You allow someone else to be designated as dealer (who decided that anyway ... tradition, the others at the table, the rules of the game, some force who controls the game, or your acceptance of it without question). The cards look old, worn, and marked to you. You are dealt your hand, and the first person to wager decides that the stakes will be life itself. You look at your hand, and see you have been given nothing of value. Is this when you decide that you have been dealt a bad hand?

Or was it before, when you decided there was only one game in town?

Or was it before, when you decided to go along with the choice of dealer?

Or was it before, when you agreed to play with the marked deck?

Or is it now, when you agree to play with such ultimate stakes?

Or is it now, when you wager at that level, even knowing the hand you hold seems unlikely to win?

Or is it now, when you stay at the table and continue to play?

Or is it in the future, when knowing what you do, you allow yourself to be beaten?

Or is it in the future, when having been beaten once, you stay in the fixed game for hand after hand?

When did life deal you a bad hand without your taking part in the process?

Yes, things can and do happen that we consider bad. It is when we consider them as happening <u>to us</u> without any participation on our part that we make ourselves victims, people without options. That is what victimhood does to people: it not only presents them with life experiences which are spirit-challenging, it also asks them to respond to those experiences in ways that are spirit-denying.

When one is a victim, when one sees life as a bad hand dealt to them, they are not only playing the bad hand but also agreeing to do nothing about it.

To me, the ultimate victimization is what we do to ourselves when we not only think of ourselves as victims but then also accept that as a given.

We then become totally shaped by externals, and lose any sense of our ability to shape life.

To what extent do you buy into the role of victim for yourself?

Others have more choices in their lives than I do.

This sounds to me like comparative victimhood.

"Others are not as put upon as much as I am."

How do you know?

The best you can see is how people express what is happening for them. You see the results more than the experiences. Unless you walk their life path, with their sense of self, you cannot know the causes that produce the results you see. And you cannot walk their life path, with their sense of self. You are you, and they are they.

As the old adage goes, "Be yourself – everyone else is taken."

But, when you compare yourself to others, you are not being yourself.

You are being yourself over-and-against-others. You are letting those others shape you and your life in the comparison.

Why are you doing that?

A long list of possibilities comes to my mind.

Is there a list that comes to your mind?

Do any of those possibilities describe some of your own feelings?

Any thoughts about where those feelings are coming from?

Any thoughts about how you might want to and could change to think about your life less in comparison with others?

To what extent do you allow yourself to be define by your perception of others?

There are some things over which I am powerless.

I participate in a number of discussions in Internet chat rooms and on Message/Discussion Boards. One of the threads of conversation that occurs with amazing (or even alarming) frequency is the notion of powerlessness. Part of what amazes me is that these various points of discussion are on topics as diverse as spirituality, railroading, politics, religion, and education. There seems to be a pervasive, international, interfaith, sub-cultural attitude of powerlessness.

Unless one is a megalomaniac, one who feels all powerful, one knows that she or he does not hold all the power in the world. We are not in control of all things.

(Indeed, we may not even be in control of many of the things we think we control!) We do not hold power and dominion over all.

In my summer visits to Ocracoke Island, part of the Outer Banks of North Carolina, I am often met at the public beach with a warning sign about rip tides. For those not familiar with ocean swimming, these can be the most fearsome movements of water in the ocean. Usually formed at a point in the beach where the water from two waves on different parts of the beach is funneled back into the larger ocean along only one path, it is a strong tide that carries everything in it seaward for great distance. You can be standing in as little water as mid-thigh high which seems placid and suddenly a rising current will sweep your feet out from under you, and in a matter of seconds you are being swept away from shore at the rate of the current, a current so strong that even the strongest Olympic swimmer cannot beat its force. You just know you are in the midst of something over which you are powerless. Many people, at the moment of that perception, panic and are frequently lost to the sea.

Does this bring to mind a life experience of your own?

Have you ever been carried by a current you felt you could not resist?

How did that feel?

Did that feeling begin to permeate your whole attitude toward life?

What did you do?

If you were struggling with that rip tide, yes, against its force you might well be powerless. Even your best efforts against the tide will gain you little against it and those same efforts will sap all of your energy until you sink into the tide. To get into a power struggle with such a force is a fruitless action.

So, what can one do?

There are three recommended responses to being in a rip tide. See if you sense a shift about powerlessness in each of them.

- As soon as you sense that you are in a current beyond the control of your own energies, you should scream for help. Admit that you cannot go it alone. You need to enlist the energy of others in facing this immense power. Alone we may be powerless, but together we may be able to prevail.
- As soon as you sense that you are in that current, stop resisting, go into a float position, ride the tide, save your strength, and when the current has weakened in the larger ocean, begin to make your way back toward shore with all of your energy intact, *making sure that you aim for a different point on the shore than the point from which you were swept away.* We may be powerless against some of life's tides, but in time they will dissipate in life's boundless sea, and we, with our energies intact, can then take up to get on with shaping our lives *as long as we don't try to go back to where we were before.*
- As soon as you sense that you are in that current, turn at right angles to the current and swim (in other words,

swim parallel to the beach). You will be swept seaward, but you will not be fighting the current. Most rip tides are fairly narrow, only a few hundred feet at most. In a relatively short time you will move yourself out of the current, and be able to set your own direction, *as long as you don't turn back into the current*. We may be powerless against some of life's tides, but if we move sideways through them instead of totally resisting them, in time we will find ourselves beyond their power. We can change our direction to find a new place in which to be powerful, *as long as we don't go back where we are powerless*.

When you are in the midst of a life moment in which you feel powerless, what do you do?

Seek connection with others with whom you can find empowerment?

Go with the flow until your energy can again allow you to shape your path?

Move in a new direction to find a new place where you can sense your power to shape your life again?

To what extent to you allow a feeling of powerlessness to render you powerless?

What happens to me in life is my own responsibility.

One of the central tenets of the emergent chaos theory is that none of us can fully understand all the factors that underlie any event. The classic reference is to the flapping of a butterfly's wings in Beijing resulting ultimately, in connection with many other seemingly unconnected events, in a hurricane along the Atlantic coast. One cannot easily know the results of any single action, and one cannot easily detect the many, apparently chaotic actions which bring about a result.

Of course, such scientific thinking is a problem in terms of prevalent religious thinking.

On the one hand, we have classic deterministic religious thinking, that what happens is all determined by a divine plan. The divine plan removes human responsibility from any actions. We are only living out "God's Will."

On the other hand, we have classic atheistic religious thinking, that there is no overall design or plan to existence, only the sum total of what just happens.

In between these two extremes, religions have carved out their own territory. Some offer a divine plan but human choice. Some offer that choice, but only in some matters. Others suggest a co-creative role for humanity, working within divine possibility. Others suggest that the creative role is human, collectively projected as if there were some divine plan. Still others argue a slow realization of a natural order which comes into being by our efforts. Still others argue a continuing revelation of the cosmic order, a revelation that can only come about through our human interaction with that cosmos.

Or, simply put, we can talk about God's will, or human choice limited by a divine plan, or a human/divine cooperative effort, or a divinity shaped by human design, or a natural law susceptible to human discovery, or a human design out of chaos. The range is wide.

If we take the one extreme, that of a controlling divine

order to existence, then it is impossible to think of being responsible for everything that happens to us in life. If we take the other extreme, that of a lack of any controlling order or design, but a participation in the purely material world, by our current scientific understandings it is impossible to think of being responsible for everything that happens to us in life. If neither complete-design nor lack-of-design can support total individual responsibility for everything that happens in life, then no combination of either can as well.

Does this make sense to you?

Then, if we think we are responsible for everything that happens to us, such thinking has to be about something else.

Is it an attempt to feel in control?

Is it an attempt to deal with feelings of guilt (which can also be a form of control of a situation over which we have no control)?

Is it an attempt to assert a questioned independence by claiming responsibility?

If you said you were responsible for everything that happened in your life, why did you say that?
If you said you were not responsible for everything that happened in your life, why did you say that?

People like me do not get a fair deal out of life.

Reclaiming the Sould of Your Faith

I have always been intrigued by news stories of complex social situations in which one group of people claim to be oppressed by a perceived ruling majority, only to themselves be seen as the oppressive majority in relation to some other group.

The feisty high school seniors who rebel against parents and faculty for perceived violations of their freedom, but who subjugate the freshmen. Warring tribes who win their independence from colonial powers only to turn around and use the same tactics against tribes who are considered inferior. The list can be endless. Blacks, Hispanics, women, young people, old people, foreigners, traditionalists, radicals, conservatives.

Listen to any of the current talk radio programs and, no matter what the philosophical bent of the program, this is the main theme: life treats "us" worse than it treats "them."

Do you believe that life itself deals differently with different people?

How? Why?

Is life a condition that happens to us, or something that we create, or help to create?

Is life to be measured against life for others?

We can only be thinking that life gives us a bad deal in comparison to what other people seem to get if we do not see ourselves as possessing a measure of independent thinking and believing. Such a comparison allows us to be shaped by the condition of others rather than our own condition. It allows others to set the expectations, the agenda, and the perceived outcome of life.

Is that what you want ... to have life's meaning primarily determined other than by yourself?

I can never hope to know what I should do.

"Should ..."

The word implies an external focus.

And, if one's notion of life is externally focused then, truly, one can never hope to know what one "should" do.

The expectations of living will always be external, foreign, even alien. If the source or sources of valuation and evaluation are separated from one, they will always remain, to some extent, unknowable and unknown.

Of course, some external expectations maybe so totally incorporated into a person that they are no longer external. But that process of incorporation requires more than blind acceptance. There has to be some interaction, some co-creative process by which the abstract becomes the realized. To be internalized, to become a "want to" rather than a "should", we have to become active agents in the transformation.

We all can, if we wish, become informed about what we "want to" do in life. We can even be hopeful about coming close to understanding most of our desires, our choices, our wants.

Which is it that you focus on? "Should" or "want to"?

Which are you seeking to understanding better, what you "should do" or what you truly, deeply "want to do"?

Life occurs according to laws which I did not make and cannot change.

Is this realism, or is this determinism (the belief that everything in life is determined outside of ourselves)?

Only you know the answer for yourself.

Is this a statement of accepting your current reality which has some limitations, some guidance by "laws" of existence? For example, you cannot fly like the birds without some mechanical assistance. You cannot breathe underwater without some aid. By accepting what are "givens" in our lives, we can stop dissipating energy in attempts to create impossible other realities.

Or is this a statement of resignation, of living as if your current sense of reality is a limitation? Think of Leonardo Da Vinci; if he had accepted the prevailing sense of the "laws" of existence, he would not have dared dream of things like flight, visual perspective, canal locks, and so much more. Galileo, Copernicus, Susan B. Anthony, Martin Luther King, Jr. ...what if each of them had accepted the seeming laws as givens, and not let their energies flow into uncharted territory? Our greatest religious leaders have always been those who have similarly seen a horizon for human life and faith beyond where prevailing wisdom set the edge of existence.

Or is this a statement of burden, of the obligation of limitation and a lack of self-direction as the nature of the universe. Do you buy into the "you are born, life is hard, and then you die" philosophy in which there is no room for change, creativity?

Acceptance, resignation, burden – how does your life

unfold for you?

How would you like it to unfold?

Some people are lucky, and some are not.

Luck?

What is luck but the wholesale assignment of control to something outside of self?

And what do we mean when we say that some people are lucky? (and some are not.)

Remember Richard Cory of poetry, the man-about-town, envied by all, who went home and put a bullet through his brain.

And the Lotto winners who in a few years are bankrupt and miserable.

And all the socialites, the stuff of "The Lifestyles of the Rich and Famous" ... how many relationships slip through the fingers of these "lucky" people.

I am reminded of the old reminiscence: "I cried because I had no shoes until I met a person who had not feet."

Using the concept of luck as a measure of how we are doing is allowing ourselves to be externally measured.

Along with that external sense of life's control and value, is the admonition: "Be careful what you wish for; you might get it." How often has the perceived "luck" of one time of your life turned unlucky through changed perceptions?

Reclaiming the Sould of Your Faith

If you wish for luck, you might get it; but that does not mean you will get a meaningful life?

I cannot choose what happens to me, but I can choose how I will react to it.

If there were one thing I would hope you would take from this chapter, maybe post on your refrigerator in bold letters, this is it!

Does it feel as significant to you?

Here is a combination of acceptance and empowerment.

I am not in control of everything. I will not delude myself into thinking that I can construct everything that will occur in my life.

But I can be in control of my reactions to everything that happens. I will choose to see that I can shape my feelings and actions through insight and understanding.

This is an ultimate acceptance that meaning can be found in any circumstance, since the meaning is in our reaction to circumstances.

Every day people in every station of life, in every culture, at every age, face the choice of finding meaning in their circumstances or not. There are not any human situations which have not yielded to some person deep, life-shaping, life-affirming meaning. And there are not any human situations which have not yielded to some person deep, life-denying, self-deprecating despair. The situations do not determine which will happen – our reactions to the situations will!

Randolph W.B. Becker

There is a purpose to life, and so I need to go with the plan.

I do not *know* if there is a purpose to life.

I think there is a purpose if we see everything that occurs as part of all-that-is, as our existence adds to that sum total.

Anything less than that universal sense of purpose becomes a matter of faith.

For example, I believe that the purpose of my life is to learn and remember such things as will help me become more fulfilled as the spiritual being that I am, so that I can find meaningful spiritual connection to other fulfilled spiritual entities in creating even more complex spiritual reality.

But, I cannot prove that this is so. I can only have the faith that it is.

No, I can do more.

I can live with that faith not as a restriction but as a liberation. Instead of worrying about that purpose as an external measure of what I "ought" to do in life, I use this model of faith as a tool I can use to open up expanding meaning in my life. Learning toward remembering becomes the means, not the obligation.

But, what of your own belief on this?
Do you believe that life has a purpose?
If not, why not?
If so, what is that purpose?

And more importantly, if you have a faith in that purpose, how does that purpose become operative in your life?

In other words, do you just believe in the purpose, or do you live the purpose?

Independent faith would ask us to have more than a faith – it would ask us to live that faith.

I can make meaning in my life.
Do you think you can make meaning in your life?

Or do you think that the best you can do is receive meaning?

Or do you think that the best you can do is live in a meaningless world?

Again, is your focus outside of yourself, or inside yourself?

If you cannot make meaning, then how meaningful would any supposed "meaning" be?

And remember, receiving meaning from outside oneself and then shaping it to one's own situation and faith is an act of meaning making. Just as raw steel made elsewhere can then be creatively shaped into I-beams, stairwell banisters, automobiles, and so much more, the raw materials of meaning become truly meaningful to us only as we creatively shape them into our lives.

How do you shape life's meaning into becoming your meaning?

This list is testing and measuring me.
Wow! Where did that come from?

Does it feel to you like life is testing you?

Does it feel to you like you are being measured against something external?

You are the one who is asking yourself these questions.

You are the one who is using this instrument as a way to think about the topic is that way.

How often do all of us re-assign our actions onto external sources? Probably most of us do this as a means of protecting ourselves, of seeing the judgment assumed as external, since otherwise we would have to understand ourselves as the most central evaluators of our lives. Something in us likes to be dependent in this way, because then we can dismiss the results as not really being accurately about us.

As we move into more independent faith, we begin to see that the best that any perspective (test, measurement, etc.) can do is provide us access to our own awareness of our own assessments. At the most independent level, we stop reading any and all of those ever-present magazine and e-zine quizzes ("What kind of closet organizer are you?", etc.) and instead use the ever-present realities of life itself as triggers for our own quizzing of ourselves. We trade in the measurements of others for our own internalized sense of evaluation.

I am seeing myself through the eyes of these statements.

Here is that sense of internalized sense of evaluation.

Reclaiming the Sould of Your Faith

These statement are seen as windows into our selves rather than as frames delineating our selves.

The focus is upon what is seen, not on the instrument of insight.

In the most independent faith there is no limit to what can provide those insights. From the most sacred scriptures to the most mundane conversation, all contacts of self with self, and self with "other," can be windows of insight. By "other" I include everything that is not one's self – books, people, nature, spirit, the divine – everything.

One with independent faith is striving to see oneself as one is, and then exploring the ways that the revealed self can fully participate in all the worlds that surround one: making meaning and sharing that meaning in the collective larger process of shared meaning making.

Shaping, not being shaped.

- - - -

I hope this long journey through thoughts about independent faith has opened some windows for you, or at least shown you where there are some windows you can decide to open.

As you follow your own path, I offer you four simple closing thoughts about independent faith:

Faith that is independent, which helps people influence institutions as opposed to being influenced by institutions places one's "locus of control" firmly within one's self. You know you have this locus when you see your faith as:

Yours – not as some representation, product, assessment of any other.

You are you!

Focused - not diffused.
Who you are is clear!
Owned - not borrowed, inherited, derived.
You have shaped and shape who you are!
Directed - not adrift.
You have a clear direction to your life!

This, then, is the seventh test of our faiths, as they are now,
and
this is the seventh criterion of the collective faith we wish to create and sustain:
Is this a model or mode that promotes our independence or our dependence?

Are we being asked to shape life, or be shaped by life?

Chapter 9
CREATIVE
Active vs. Static

Picture with me these two images:

First is a great plateau, shoved upwards from the plain many years ago, and now standing in the elements as time passes. What happens to that plateau? The winds slowly erode away the top of the plateau ever so slightly. The rains come and wash away the top soil, taking with the growing downhill stream more and more of the heights. Rivulets become gullies become rivers become gorges become canyons. The plateau is wearing away. Each step of the way passive transformation is taking place. Without some force to push it upward again or to build upon it as a base, the plateau will, in the fullness of time, become the plain again, its identity lost into the sameness of everything else. It was created, but now that creation is being lost. It is a breaking apart.

Second is a small seed, lying warmly in moist soil, taking into itself energy and transforming that energy from its various forms – light, water, soil – into a rapidly multiplying set of cells, differentiating into roots, stem, then leaves, stalk, then flower and eventually more seeds. Each step of the way an act of active transformation is taking place. What was created is creating more. It is a coming together.

Which would you rather be, that plateau or that seed?

Now, think about these two religious positions:

First, that you are the product of a creative act, and as

Reclaiming the Sould of Your Faith

such the best you can do is try to maintain what was created. However, you exist in an environment which is filled with forces that will attempt to wear down, break apart what was created. Some would even say that in the very act of coming into existence, you were born with one strike against you. A passive transformation occurred to you simply by becoming human. Some portion of your positive nature was already altered. And in your contact with the world around you, you will find again and again that you will be tested just by trying to stand your ground. Forces beyond your making and control will wear away whatever goodness of creation you have ... and it will happen **to** you. The best that religion can do is try to keep you from getting too much worse.

Or second, you are the continuing co-product of both the act of creation through which you became this physical being and your own active living. You were created with a wide range of capabilities and possibilities, all of which can be fulfilled more or less depending on the way in which you approach your life. Active transformations await your every moment. In your contact with the world around you, you will find that you are sufficient to meet any challenges that come your way, and that through your actions you not only can stand your ground, but you can also move toward visionary goals of more humane living. Things, ideas, relationships come into being **through** you. Religion assists you by helping you express more of your own creative possibility.

Which would you rather be, a passive product or an active co-creator?

One of the laws of thermodynamics is that any system, over time, will tend to wind down *unless there is some infusion of new energy into the system.* This is usually spoken of as entropy.

In common usage, entropy has come to mean that "things fall apart." Entropy makes Murphy's Law ("If something can go wrong, it will!") seem so prevalent.

Take a house, for example.

Someone builds a house, puts on the shutters, paints the clapboards, shingles the roof, lays in the sod, and calls it home. It looks wonderful.

But, in five years, it will not look as wonderful unless someone puts in energy (work, time, materials) in its upkeep.

Just keeping things as they are takes a tremendous amount of energy.

Being static, trying to keep things as they are, takes work!

In a universe in which things are always coming and going, to stand still in the force of the gales of change is to invest energy, tremendous energy.

I served a church in the historic district on the east side of Providence, Rhode Island. The stated intent of the historic district was to keep all the properties therein consistent with their historic identity. Never mind that over 200 years creative people had changed colors, installed central heating, and so much more, and never mind that over 200 years of settling, fires, wear-and-tear had taken its toll, and never mind that over 200 years some original materials had become impossible to obtain or others recognized as unsafe: the buildings were to be kept as static as possible.

I can remember meeting after meeting of the governing board, the Prudential Committee, investing great energy into meeting the expectations for remaining static.

However, lest we assume this is an issue about history, a congregation I served in Massachusetts had a striking modern building, and they invested equal energy in trying to keep their modernism static.

Individuals also fall under the spell of stasis, keeping things the way they are.

At the most benign level, perhaps, the college student comes home at the first first-year break and spends great time re-arranging the bedroom back to its familiar patterns, and visits old haunts from high school.

At the mid-life crisis point, many people decide to finally go to those reunions, or contact long lost friends, in an attempt to nail down some piece of their lives, make it static.

And in the times of great life loss, it is common for people to invest great energy in trying to keep static was has been revealed as transitory: keeping the dead person's bedroom unchanged for years; setting an extra place at the dinner for the person who will no longer be eating; continuing to use plurals when now only singulars will work. I know about this: I have gone that route myself, trying to static in the times of my life what has changed into timelessness.

You have probably met couples (are you in this kind of relationship?) in which tremendous energy is spent in maintaining the relationship as it was "when we first met." All the changes of life are forgotten in an attempt to make static the magic moments of initial endearment (and lost are all the magic moments that could have transpired as two people grow together through life's infinite revelation).

Many people try to hold life and its many elements as constants, as static pieces of the ever-changing equation. Religions, growing up from individual longings for continuity, create structures in which continuity becomes ultimately important. "Who was, is, and evermore shalt be, world without end."

Yet, think about all the energy it takes to do that.

A moving plaque at the bridge in Concord, Massachusetts, where the battle took place whose shots were "heard round the world" speaks of the dead British soldiers who died that day "to keep the past upon its throne."

What is the alternative?

Let's think back to that new house.

In fact, let's look back to a whole neighborhood of new houses. Levittown, on Long Island, was one of those fabled developments created after World War II, to provide housing for the returning troops. You have probably seen the aerial views of Levittown, with street after street of houses looking exactly the same. Simple, mass-produced, cookie-cutter homes. Jokes arose about such towns, about husbands coming home and entering what was thought to be home, and ending up in someone else's house, and not noticing the error for hours. Beneath the surface was a less jovial reality of racially exclusive covenants and other socially manipulative measures. However, looking solely at the housing, we had a whole community of brand new houses.

If one returns to Levittown today, it is hard to believe that all the houses began looking the same. The few homes that have remained static, simply maintained in their original color and configuration, look horribly out of date, almost unkempt. Most homes, with the application of new siding, different colors, additions of all types, have taken on individuating identities.

Now, yes, it would seem cheaper and easier to keep the houses exactly as they were in the beginning, and not engage in the creative process of modification and modernization. Yet, think about this a moment. The original houses had wooden clapboard siding, needing repainting on a regular basis. The original shutters, also wood, needed even more attention. Add in the wooden sash windows and separately hung storm windows and screen. Then, inside the house, think about maintaining the original appliances, the outdated plumbing, the potential dangerously deteriorating and under-rated electrical systems.

By contrast, think of the houses that were adapted over time, clad in relatively maintenance-free siding and shutters, with full storm/screen vinyl window units, with updated electrical and plumbing system matched to new, more energy efficient and user-friendly appliances.

If one analyses the two types of houses, taking into account the initial cost, cost of maintenance, cost of improvements, and present value, the houses that stayed static have lost value relative to the houses that have been changed. The energy of materials, time, effort, and money invested into the creative transformation of those homes has actually created more value than standing still does.

Is this also true of our lives?

I suspect you intuitively know the answer to this.

You know how much more energy it takes to be defensive as compared to being open and un-threatened.

You know the old adage, "If you need someone to help you, ask the busy person, who is the only one who has the time," which affirms the notion that those who use resources of life find an abundance of such resources.

Perhaps one of the best examples and experiences of this in life is love. If one tries to live within oneself, to preserve the energy of life within the circle of a single life, the most that one gets is oneself, and even that is unlikely, as few people find themselves complete enough, in themselves, to meet all of their needs. But, when one is willing to use the energy necessary to reach outward from oneself, and to connect to another reaching outward from their self, it is as if a great reservoir of energy is suddenly opened for both the self and the other.

Have you experienced that yourself?

Have you known a time when you did invest your emotional or physical energy in some way that was unexplored, risky, creative, only to find that a small amount of your energy liberated a vast field of other energy?

What happened? How did it feel?

From my many conversations with people about especially powerful moments in their lives, they overwhelming speak about such times, even when those times are associated with loss as well as with perceived gains.

It is probably easy to imagine people who have decided to be active and creative finding new energy by pursuing that decision when they are focusing on some desired goal.

But, over and over again, people who have moved along the path of grief tell me they worried about allowing too much energy to go toward grieving ("I thought I would lose what little energy I had if I used it to grieve.") only to discover that they found more meaning, understanding, and ability to move ahead in life than they could have imagined. When grief is invested in, the energy released for living can be awesome.

Creativity (the act of combining into being and meaning what before was only available as potential resident in separate elements) uses energy to reveal more energy.

Stasis, the act of keeping things as they are, simply uses energy.

Now, what would all of this mean to your faith?

If your faith were to be seen as a house, is it a house that you try to maintain as it was when it was created, or is it a house that has been creatively adapted over the years?

Are there some faith components that you are only willing to maintain, but never to question?

What would happen if you were to invest some energy in opening your most central points of faith to examination, to questioning, and perhaps even inclusion in a wider expression of the inherent values if not the specifics of that faith point?

Dr. Gabriel Moran, the essayist on religious development, has postulated that the pre-requisite to a deeper level of faith is a full and open doubt. Faith is born out of a doubt that allows everything to be creatively questioned in a way that revelation becomes possible once again. When we are not busy defending the static, the known, we can be open to the awesome "aha" moments out of which living faith arises.

The *Faith Development In The Adult Life Cycle* project of Dr. Kenneth Stokes, using its national, inter-faith survey of United States faith patterns, found that people who could describe their faith in the strongest terms across the many years of their lives admitted to recurring times of such intense doubting and questioning. Invariably these respondents told of finding new, more powerfully compelling faithing after being open to radically and creatively considering their previous faith down to its core.

Is there some element in your own faith that you think you could not open to such doubt, such questioning, and maybe such more inclusive expression?

Why?

Do you find yourself having to defend that element of faith? To others? To yourself?

What do you think would happen if you were to question that element?

Consider this:
If it is an element of faith that has roots in the basic structure of the universe, how could you lose it by opening yourself to its examination?

If it is not an element of faith that has roots in the basic structure of the universe, why would you want to keep that part of your faith static?

Yet, keeping faith static appears to be the very core of religion. Religion seems to be more concerned with people having a faith as opposed to people being faithful.

Let me unwrap this a bit more.

When religions, in general, speak of faith, they speak of living as if a certain set of doctrines were materially true. For religion, faith is an object more than a process. One possesses the object, the faith, and like any treasured object, one protects that faith. It is almost like religious faith were some kind of antique, which if it came into your possession you would not dare to cut into, repaint, dissect, or maybe desecrate by contact with profane elements. Your possession would require that you maintain that object but keep it inviolate – static.

I bet you know of people who live their lives like this. Just like those relatives who had such "valuable" furniture that it was always covered with tightly fitted see-through vinyl, people who *have* a faith worry more about protecting it than experiencing it, just as they have a life-style they need to protect more than a life. Indeed, they seem more possessed by that faith, like some energy-demanding obligation, than possessing it for themselves as a resource.

Then you probably knew some other relative who would welcome you into the house with a sweeping gesture while saying "Hey, I know its not fancy, but just find yourself a place that fits you, and be comfortable." That same person probably taught you how to delight not just in the impressive, valuable things, but in the simple, seeming valueless things. That person probably seemed more concerned with living life than having a life-style.

Well, the same can be said in the realm of faith. Faithful people are those who are less concerned with having a specific faith and more interested with trying to live lives that encompasses the process of moving in faith. One senses that these are people sustained by a faith that is never captured in one place, but which is always reaching for more inclusive understandings. Their faith does not ask for allegiance or obedience, but searches for experience and expression.

A faith that is creative is a faith that is active, trying to experience and express spiritual values that are always in the process of creation.

What do you perceive as the creative edges of your faith?

Reclaiming the Sould of Your Faith

How will you be active in moving in that direction?

Exactly!

How will you be active in moving in that direction?

Let me suggest one model for keeping faith active rather than static.

And it is a model that does not require you to forsake your present faith in a wholesale manner. To essentially doubt your faith does not mean that you abandon those values that sustain you, but rather that you consider them as points in a process which can reveal an even more inclusive and universal set of values (which in turn is itself only made up of points in a process). Your faith becomes a starting point from which to actively reach out, not an end point upon which to sit statically.

The method I have found that works for many people is to encourage them to become more familiar with the faiths of as many other people as they can. Note, I do not say to become familiar with the religions of as many other people as they can, for religion is a formalized, impersonal representation of static faith.

Rather, I am suggesting that one tries to interact with as diverse a group of people as possible, and with those people both risk sharing one's own deepest understandings of faith and ask them about theirs. Share what inspires you, not as fact but as faith. Inquire of others what inspires them, and listen to their responses also as faiths to be understood rather than facts to be debated,

AND

<u>look for connections, not differences.</u>

Try to discover how your own faith connects with the

faith of others to disclose an even larger pattern of faith.

Be open to being changed in the process.

Again, remember that faith is not a possession but a tool. Make your faith a tool that increasingly can respond to evermore universal challenges and understandings.

And take heart – all that you now truly hold in faith will still be included in the enhanced faith you will create ... nothing is lost, but much is built upon. What you once thought was the answer becomes the basis for questions you could not even imagine before. Where you once thought you had reached an end-point in discerning the wonders of creation, now you will see you were only standing before another door awaiting your willingness to open it. Who you once thought foreign or even heretical will now become a companion on the path of spiritual discovery. Why things happen, once expressed as certainties and formula, will now become possibilities and conjectures which work to explain until an even larger understanding is embraced. When all of this will happen stops being a matter of external forces, and now becomes the product of our own inner commitment to active faith.

What does this one model for an active faith suggest to you?

What do you think, feel, fear, or hope would happen if you were to have such an active faithing?

How would you begin?

As Hillel wrote: "If not now, when?"

This, then, is the eighth test of our faiths, as they are now,

Reclaiming the Sould of Your Faith

and

this is the eighth criterion of the collective faith we wish to create and sustain:

Is this a model or mode that promotes that which is active or that which is static?

Are we being asked to be creative, or just created?

Chapter 10
ACCESSIBLE - REASONABLE
Evident vs. Secret/Mysterious

This will be the shortest chapter in this book.
Four simple concepts:

    A faith that is truly your own, full of the qualities we have already discussed, does not rely on big words or fancy arguments.

    A faith that is truly your own does not ask you to make a leap of faith to get to your leaps of faith.

    A faith that is truly yours is not mysterious to you.

    A faith that is truly yours can be explained by you in your own language, filled with images from your own experiences.

A faith that is truly your own, full of the qualities we have already discussed, does not rely on big words or fancy arguments.

If I have been successful in writing this book, you have not needed to consult a dictionary to understand what I have shared. You have not needed to find an encyclopedia. The concepts presented have been very evident on the face of them. They either made sense to you or they did not.

Has that been your experience with this book?

If one turns to the typical book on religious thought, one finds words and phrases like teleology, eschatology, cosmogony, transubstantiation, vicarious atonement, pre- or post-millennialism. (Please, don't rush to look these up

... they are only big words to obscure concepts, concepts which if they were explained totally would still baffle most of us.)

A question – if faith is a tool we use to live out our ordinary lives, what usefulness is any complex theory that is removed from our everyday living? If you want to work on a home project and need a tool, you don't want one that comes with a necessary 200-page instruction manual and a required three-year course of study for its use. Why do we allow the tool of faith to be treated any differently?

A faith that is truly your own does not ask you to make a leap of faith to get to your leaps of faith.

As I read so many books about religion, or listen to various speakers on faith, I am always amazed how many of them want to add a layer onto faith.

Faith, by its nature, is that tool which allows us to live as if something were true even without absolute proof. Through the vehicle of faith, we find we can proceed into a fuller expression of life than if we had to wait for all things to be proven. Often the proof follows the faith, as our ability to move forward through faith then brings us to a place where the faith reveals its own proof. (As they say, "The proof is in the pudding, not in the recipe.")

But, what many religions ask you to is to accept one more step of faith ... take something else, first, without proof, before you can get to your own leap of faith toward truth. Maybe it is the requirement that one accept on faith the validity of a certain book, a particular religious figure, or a specific religious event. Rather than focusing on the message of the book, the figure, or the event, what is requested is preliminary acceptance on faith of something else.

Sometimes it is a call to accept in faith the authority of the person promoting that faith.

There is nothing in true faith that needs to come before that faith!

A faith that is truly yours is not mysterious to you.

Yes, that faith may be awesome, amazing, moving ... and all the adjectives that inadequately express the personal experience of faith ... but when you move in faith, it is not mysterious. True faith, by its very definition, is as true and evident as anything else in life.

However, how many times have you heard someone tell you that some element of faith must remain a mystery until you are ready to have it revealed to you?

How often has someone else claimed you needed to accept that real faith will not be evident to you, because "God works in mysterious ways." If you experience it, it is hardly mysterious. And if you do not experience it, how can it be part of your faith? Perhaps we could say, "God works in ways which previously would have seemed mysterious," and that would say exactly what I am trying to say. Faith that is yours speaks to that which might have previously been mysterious, but which now is as true as anything else.

And when someone tells you they hold a special secret of faith, ask them how it can be a secret if they know it.

A faith that is truly yours can be explained by you in your own language, filled with images from your own experiences.

Some of the most eloquent expressions of faith I have received were from people who would be described as "just plain folks." They have spoken to me about life and love and loss, about beauty, joy, sorrow, and a sense of personal worth. They have told me these things accompanied by stories from their lives.

Some of the least eloquent expressions of faith I have heard have been in the classrooms of theological schools, in gatherings of clergy, on the pages of religious books. These are often long statements of theories about obscure elements of existence, usually accompanied by long footnotes and reference to other long statements of theories about equally obscure elements of existence.

The faith you find through your own experience (and by experience I mean not just the events of your life but also the thoughts of your mind) can be perfectly expressed in your own words. Never apologize for how you speak of your faith if it is truly yours!

This, then, is the ninth test of our faiths, as they are now,

and

this is the ninth criterion of the collective faith we wish

Randolph W.B. Becker

to create and sustain:

Is this a model or mode that is evident or secret and mysterious?

Are we being asked to be have faith in that which is accessible and reasonable, or a faith in that which is obscure and theoretical?

Chapter 11
SPIRITUAL
Spiritual vs. Material

When you read the word "religion" what comes to mind? Try this exercise. Have someone say the word "religion" to you, and write down the first word or phrase that comes to mind. Then, have them say the word again, and record what comes next. And so on. (If you are alone, an alternative would be to write down the word "religion" between each of your responses.) And do this before you continue to read further in this chapter.

Go ahead ... this book will wait.

OK – if you have done this, you will have a list of words that describes religion to you.

Take a look at this list. How many of the words describe "things"? By things, I mean the obvious physical things (buildings, people, books, etc.) **and** I also mean the less obvious things which gain their definition by reason of some quantification (congregations, journeys, creeds).

So, on your list, how many things are there? And how many non-things.

If you are like most of the people I meet in workshops, you will find that your responses are full of things, and nearly void of non-material entries.

Now, a second exercise.

Make a list of what you would like to get out of your association with religion (assuming the association to be a positive one).

Yes, make the list!

Now, look at this second list. Do the same analysis.

If you are like most of the people I meet, this list will be the exact opposite of the first list – it will be full of non-material things. Some of the terms I hear over and over again are: joy, peace, fulfillment, connection, love, meaning, acceptance, forgiveness, support.

So, why do we turn to material institutions in search of spiritual experiences?

Probably because we have a prevailing cultural image of the physical being primary and the spiritual being secondary. We see the spiritual as the result, not the cause.

But, it has never really been that way!

All of the institutions of religion are the outgrowth of spiritual experiences. The feelings of individuals came first, followed by some form in which those feelings were expressed so that others might also appreciate them. The spiritual became material.

The longest standing spiritual traditions, those of native tribal populations, have always had a spiritual connection with the earth which denies the ownership of the earth by any person or people. Others, in seeking to remember the experience of that early spirituality, have sought to find special power in certain places on the earth that are then named and owned as sacred.

The long tradition of Hinduism brings together the spiritual insights and experiences of generations beyond number. To make the insights of people long since lost beyond even memory available to the living, images representing the experiences have taken form.

The great enlightened one, the Buddha, spoke beneath a bo tree about a life beyond attachment to material things. Others, wanting to follow as spiritually as possible, sat beneath the same tree, or beneath other similar trees, in his same pose.

Lao-Tzu experienced the constant interplay of the elements of life as a great balance. Others, wanting to be reminded of his insights, created the symbolic yin-yang ☯.

Moses, confronting the slavery of the Jews by the Pharaoh of Egypt, invoked a highly spiritual moment in the night of the first Passover. Others, wanting to experience and understand the same spiritual elements of redemption and freedom, observe the traditional Seder meal.

Jesus, in his ministry, assembled his closest friends together for a Seder Meal on the first night of Passover, and in the middle of that meal shared his vision for how they would continue to relate even if he were no longer in their midst. Others, wanting to remember that last night of his public ministry, use the same elements of bread and wine.

Mohammed, in his vision of a force of the divine which stretches across all ethnic and tribal boundaries, focused on the eternal east. Others, wanting to summon to mind his great spirit, have located the east in certain places where Mohammed lived and specific places significant in his ministry.

The division of the Western and Eastern Catholic churches, the Protestant Reformation, the growth of New Age religions ... they all began as initial spiritual experiences or understandings of individuals. Others, wanting to capture the same insights and spiritual experiences, adopted words, symbols, methods, modes, and even names to be representative of the new faith. Married or un-married clergy; Easter's date figured by the new moon and full moon or only the full moon; a crucifix or a cross; a grail or a chalice or a cup; leavened or unleavened bread; yoga or transcendental meditation; crystals or amulets. The spiritual experiences have been transformed into material expressions, and material expressions that divide people and beliefs and spiritual experiences in the process.

How do we keep ourselves doing the same thing?
At one level, we cannot. And at the same time, we can.

Randolph W.B. Becker

If the experiences of our lives are so profound that they are transformed in us into faith, if what those experiences provoke in us become tools by which we live out the rest of our lives, we have already begun the process of materializing the spiritual. We will, through our faith, take senses, intuitions, feelings, notions, and other by-products of experiences and find some way to express the inexpressible. The struggle of every spiritual person, the mystical challenge, is how to make real in life what is felt in spirit. We want the ecstasy of the experience to take up residence in our lives. So, we give it form, substance, symbol, name – some form of quantity.

In fact, it would be impossible for us to recall any of those experiences without some cues, some tangible ways of remembering them. They are ethereal, like sounds drifting over distant waves of light, and we want to make a recording or take a picture, so we can remember what our heart and mind and spirit have no way to capture forever.

The trick is how to focus on what the remembered cues mean, not on the cues themselves.

If we cannot help transforming faith-informing experiences into some level of material reality, we can strive to be conscious about that transformation and seek to always remember the spiritual experience, not the material reminders.

I have found that these five guidelines help people remain mindful of the difference between the spiritual and the ways we represent and remember the spiritual.

Do you turn to material things in place of seeking spiritual experiences?

In the congregation in the upper Midwest that I served as a student minister, I had a parishioner who was one of the most active members of the congregation ... or what I should say was that this person was always in motion. I would arrive and the door would have been opened, the walkway swept or shoveled (depending on the season), the heat adjusted, the chairs set up, the lights on, etc. As the morning would progress, this person would greet newcomers, usher, get the coffee ready, and do what seemed like a thousand other things.

When I had the opportunity to call on this person, in the course of conversation I was surprised by this comment: "You know, when I first got involved with the congregation having something to do made me feel connected, you know, and so I just kept doing it all because that reminds me of how I felt so connected when I first came. But when I hear all of these other people talk about their spirituality, I don't know what they mean. I feel so disconnected from what is happening in the congregation."

I suggested a simple course of treatment ... "Let me find some other people to do some of those jobs, and just come to services for a month or two. Don't do anything, just be."

Well, those first few weeks were hard ... a big transition from material connection to a seeming non-connection. But then in one service, I looked over and saw closed eyes and the glint of a tear in the corner of one of them, the sun shining down on my friend. Afterwards nothing was put into words ... just one of the biggest hugs I have ever received in my professional life.

Most of us do not have as dramatic a material-spiritual conversion, but we have our own moments of truth. In a time of turmoil, we grab for the well-worn Bible or Koran, as if the book itself will save us from some imagined or real threat ... when it is the wisdom there that we have found expressed in our own experiences that can resonate with our heart and spirit.

Or we have found some place, our own sense of *Walden*, where we can feel at one with the whole of the universe. We plan our vacations around that place, forgetting it is our feelings in that place that are revelatory, not the place itself. If we are *independent* and *creative* as we have discussed, then we know that it is not the place that shapes us, but rather we that shape ourselves in *that* place <u>and anywhere else we may choose to feel the same way</u>.

Or it could be a repeated prayer, a sacred icon, a touchstone, a piece of music ... any concrete thing that begins to take on a life larger than its own reality because we invest our memories in *it*, rather than in our memories; invest our ability to experience in *it*, rather than in our ability to experience.

And do not assume that this is true only of those times when we are stressed. I have known many people who only knew how to deal with joy, with pleasure, with fulfillment by placing it into some form of material context ... almost like they wanted to be assured that they would not be overwhelmed by it. But, spiritual experience, when it is genuine, is supposed to overwhelm you!

If you do not know how to experience the spiritual in the high times *and* the low times without recasting them into material terms, how can you expect to be in touch with spiritual understandings in the ordinary times, when such spiritual understandings have the capacity to make the ordinary extra-ordinary?

So, as you turn to those material reminders of spiritual experiences or spiritual desires, be mindful of what you are doing. Ask yourself, "What am I seeking to remember or experience?" and then let the material reminders go ... *focus on the spiritual aspect.*

Do you try to repeat your deepest spiritual experiences?

William James, in his groundbreaking work <u>Varieties of Religious Experience</u>, noted that one of the hallmarks of the personal spiritual experience was its unique quality: it cannot be replicated. You can't have exactly the same spiritual experience twice. No matter how much you attempt to control the factors, you can't control everything. And all of those factors would be material ones, since to control something it has to be quantifiable - unless you can measure it how can you control it?

So, in trying to repeat spiritual experiences, one is trying to use material means, including control, to gain access to that which is essential non-material and uncontrollable.

This does not mean that we cannot have similar experiences, but we need to respect the uniqueness of each of our deeply spiritual experiences.

As I write this, I am reminded of one of my own deeply spiritual experiences, experienced while I was listening to a particular piece of music. It left me feel intimately and completely at one with the whole of all existence. For many years, I went back to that piece, wishing, hoping, trying to have that same feeling. Nope. Never got there again ... until in the midst of another piece of music I again felt intimately and completely at one with the whole of all existence, in a similar but not the same experience. And then I have felt something similar in the glimpse of a sunset across the desert. And so it goes; when I try to repeat the experience I miss it, but when I remain open in other moments of life, it comes unbidden, in similar but not duplicate moments.

The challenge is to recognize when we are ritualizing a chosen path toward perceived spirituality. We then need to remember that such rituals are attempts to control circumstances, a control which does not offer any assurance of spiritual experience. However, we can focus on the spiritual experiences we have had, savor them in wordless wonder and appreciation, and strive to be radically open as opposed to ritualistically controlled ... *focus on the spiritual element.*

Do you try to measure your spiritual experiences?

A cartoon from the late 1960s shows two gurus who,

having meditated for most of their lives, sit facing each other. One of them is saying, "If you think that is an insight, wait to you hear what was revealed to me."

This cartoon was (is) funny because we have this notion of sacred people as being non-competitive. Spiritual people are not supposed to need to say, "My spiritual experience is better than yours."

Of course they wouldn't, because that would quantify the experiences. Another of the hallmarks of a spiritual experience or understanding is that it holds its own value (intrinsic), not related to value of or given by other things (extrinsic).

Has this been true for you?

Have you had a spiritual experience? Is there any way you could assign it a value? (Picture yourself with scorecards like they use at skating events ... could you hold up 7.4, or 6.8 ... would this make sense?)

True, not all spiritual experiences are the same ... but the difference is not measurable in terms that we can reduce to common language.

Yet, I keep meeting people who come to me with concerns about their spiritual life, and they compare their spiritual life in some way ... to their own past experiences, to their own expectations, or to the perceived spiritual lives of others.

Does this ring a bell for you?

Some come to me because they are deeply troubled by what they see as a decline in their spiritual lives. They talk at length about the peak experiences of their lives in the past tense. Now, what they are experiencing is not living up to their past. I begin talking with them not about their faith nor about their spiritual lives. I begin to talk to them about life in general. I ask them to tell me about their lives for the past 10 or 20 years. They pour out a long history of changes in location, family style, health, sexuality, personal needs, and so much more. I ask them how they feel about all of these things. And then I ask them if they would like to go back to some point 10 or 20 years before. Almost no one wants to go back; most people, even in their toughest times, would rather be where they are than to have to go through "all that" again. Then, I ask them if they would like to go back 10 or 20 years in their spiritual lives. And at that point the light bulb in their mind goes *click*. I can see it in their eyes. They generally have spent 10 or 20 years working on changing material realities but have not done any work on changing spiritual realities. From there we can begin a conversation.

Is this a conversation you need to have?
What do you need to say to yourself?

Another group of people come to me, and they tell me about how their spiritual life has *never* lived up to their expectations. Again, I spend time talking about how life unfolds, and then based on what I hear, I will proceed to explore one of two concepts with them: spirituality and expectation *or* spirituality and control. Together we have a conversation about the conflict between spirituality and expectations or control, since both of these are matters of quantified life, an expression of materialism.

Is this a conversation you need to have?

Reclaiming the Sould of Your Faith

What do you need to say to yourself?

The last group that I meet with are people who come with a book under their arm. It may be a classic work of spirituality or a contemporary best seller. What they tell me is that they are troubled by their inability to either get into these books or have the experiences suggested in these books. The book of the moment is often not their first book of such spiritual struggle. For some of them, it is like a spiritual method of the month club process, with a new methodology tried with each new book. For others, it is a long-standing living argument with a single book, stretching over decades.

With these people, I ask them to describe a book that they think would help them ... what is the problem with the book(s) they have brought to discuss? And they, almost without exception, can tell me about what they would like to find in a book with which they would not need to compete. After listening to them for what is usually a long time, I begin to have a conversation with them about how they would go about living up to the book they have just described, and again *click*. They come to see that the only book worth paying attention to in spirituality is the book of one's own life. Other books (including this one) can at best, in sharing experiences of others, help us to focus on our own experiences. When we compete with the insights of others, we turn their spiritual experiences *and* our own spiritual experiences material.

Is this a conversation you need to have?

What do you need to say to yourself?

If you have found that one of these scenarios has caused you to have a conversation with yourself, I hope you find yourself saying to yourself ... *focus on the spiritual*.

Do you try to generalize your spiritual experiences?

Remember back in one of the opening chapters there was a diagram of how religions reduce the whole of all-that-is down to a manageable piece, and then project that small fragment of reality as if it were the whole?

Another definition of a manageable piece of all-that-is would be a piece that you can experience in such a way that you can both recognize and appreciate it. A piece that is too small brings nothing new and special to us. Such a piece would simply show us again what we already know. A piece that is too big will overwhelm us to such an extent that we either do not experience it or we cannot appreciate what we experience. It is almost like the three bears, looking for those pieces of all-that-is that are "just right".

Any piece that is "just right" for us at our level of spiritual awareness will necessarily be less than the whole. So, if we take a single spiritual experience and generalize from it, we have to add something to that experience to make it fill out a bigger picture. What we add will necessarily be material, for it does not arise out of spiritual experience but out of our own input to the experience, which is a quantifying process of mind.

Instead of taking the small piece of all-that-is that we experience spiritually and try to project it, why not take that piece and try to inspect it ... look into it with all the spirit and openness we can muster? Once again, a simple suggestion: instead of trying to stamp the material world with a form made from of a small, single spiritual piece of all-that-is ... *follow the spiritual.*

Do you demand that others express their spiritual experiences in ways you can understand?

One of the ways that we deny spiritually-based faith is to demand that it adhere to material guidelines. Think of how you would feel if someone demanded that you explain your experience of spirit so they could understand it, *as if it were their own experience.*

Actually, you can't do it. Again, if William James' research is to be believed, spiritual experiences do not lend themselves to adequate transmission in language or other symbol systems. All you do is introduce extraneous elements into the spiritual experience, introduce material elements since language is a material system.

One of the ways that we open ourselves to a more spiritual faith is to allow others to also live within their own spiritual faiths. How do you do that?

You ask them about their spiritual experiences, and whatever they say, you accept without demand for clarification. You accept that they are trying their best to tell you. Look instead for their affect, how remembering the experience plays out in their appearance. If you are sensitive, see if you can feel their spirit, being in touch with them spiritually.

In other words, forget your need to know ... *follow the spiritual*.

And in time, when you follow the spiritual, you will discover that you will have less need to strive to convert the spiritual into the material. Those religious systems which rely heavily on material representations will drift away from you, becoming less and less relevant to you. Your own sense of faith, however, by becoming more thoroughly spiritual and by respecting the spiritual nature of the faith of others, will seem more intimate.

At the fullest development of a faith that is spiritual, all the material aspects will fall away. At that moment, when your faith is not represented by objects, thoughts, designs, and control, your faith becomes fully your own – your own as experience, your own as meaning, your own in understanding, your own in spirit.

This, then, is the final test of our faiths, as they are now,

and

this is the final criterion of the collective faith we wish to create and sustain:

Is this a model or mode that is spiritual or material?

Are we being asked to be have faith that is fully, spiritually our own, or someone else's?

Chapter 12
OUR PATHS INTO THE FUTURE

The education theorist, Thomas Groome, suggests that education is a six-movement process, not simply a moment of learning. The first five of those movements, in my own words, are:

1. An invitation to an idea, a concept, a notion, a "learning" possibility. I have tried to invite you to not only consider the state of faith in our collective lives but also to consider your own personal faith. Along the way, you have been invited to consider your personal faith ... to what extent is it:

- ☺ open
- ☺ connected
- ☺ unitary
- ☺ hopeful
- ☺ freeing
- ☺ contemplative
- ☺ independent
- ☺ creative
- ☺ accessible and reasonable
- ☺ spiritual?

2. Naming our own knowing. You have been asked to consider, recognize, name, and own your thoughts, feelings, experiences, and questions about each of these areas of faith. In naming your own faithing, you began the process of reclaiming your faith as your own. Even where there are doubts and questions, in naming those doubts and questions you have reclaimed them as your own growing edges of faith.

3. Finding common ground. From all that has been shared by me and by you we began to build understandings, areas of agreement. What appears to be common human experience? What can we say to one another that can be recognized as familiar, even if not in the exact same words or symbols? Most importantly, we have looked for common questions, shared growing edges of faith. We have enlarged the sphere of our knowing by being open to the knowing of others.

4. Sharing the community vision and story. I have hoped, through the structure and material of this book, to suggest that there is a vision and story about faith, a vision and a story which is often obscured by religion and religious institutions. I have tried to share some of that vision and story through recollected tales and personalities of religion, histories of other ordinary people, and experiences of my own life. These visions and stories form a foundation, both within inherited religion and courageous individual faith, for asking some profound questions.

5. Dialogue and dialectic – talking about the ways

in which the longings of our hearts and spirits are in sympathy or tension with the shared community vision and story. You have been asked to consider, all along the way, how you see yourself in relation to the questions being asked. Does what you experience and feel and know, or does what religion tells you one should experience and feel and know, make more sense to you?

If we were to stop at this point, this would be a theoretical book. As Tom Groome points out, real education is never theoretical. You can't learn by theory, only by practice. So, the last point in the process:

6. So what and now what? If the process we have shared in this book means anything, you will begin to have a notion of how this matters and what you are going to do about it. You will know what you have learned (about your self, about all-that-is, about your faith) when you see your living and your faithing changed in some way. Remember, affirming your faith to a greater extent is one form of change ... so this is not simply about altering what you hold in faith but also about how you hold it in faith.

Does this six-fold path to learning make sense to you?
How have you experienced these points in this book?
Have you felt any changes that you would call learning according to this model?

A concept I want to suggest at this point is a simple contrast: learning and remembering. If we are going to be concerned with "So what and now what," I think it is important to look deeper into the what of "what".

If the "what" is only learning, we need to be conscious of how many people spend their lives learning; unfortunately, it is often the same thing that is learned, over and over again. We all know how children often learn to do or not do this or that over and over again. One day they promise they know something, but the next day they don't remember it again. Learned, but not remembered. But, that process does not stop with the end of childhood.

In some of the workshops I run, I ask people about what has been the hardest thing for them to learn. After the usual banter about calculus, Arabic, and so forth, we get into other areas of frustrated learning.

"I wish I could learn," one man said, "to truly forgive and forget. I always think I will forget when I forgive, but then I don't."

A woman hesitantly said, "I wish I could learn to be more trusting."

A couple, together, said, "How to love."

What is it that you wish you could learn, truly learn?

What do you keep finding yourself learning over and over and over again?

The addition of remembering makes the learning complete. In remembering, we are talking about taking onto and into ourselves the learning in such a way that we no longer have to consider it. It is not a process of thought and option, but rather part of the fabric of our being. We have in-*corpo*-rated it ... made it part of our very self. Just as we do not have to think about breathing or making our heartbeat, we do not have to think about this – it becomes an essential part of us.

The educational process begun in this book points to a "so what and now what" where "what" is a remembered sense of faith that incorporates the ten elements through which your faith becomes your own, becomes vital, becomes vibrant. The "what" is your reclaiming the soul of your faith in such a way that you truly remember it. The ten concepts of faith move from being theory into practice in your life in ways that make sense to you, **and** they function in your life in a consistent, regular way.

Would that feel good to you?
Would you like to have the qualities of such a personal faith be part of the very fabric of your being and living?

If "yes", then the "what" of "So what" is known.
Now what?

It is at this very point in many books on faith, self-help, and religion that I feel let down. Why?

Because after espousing a theory of diversity and openness, of new directions and dimensions, the author will suddenly produce a single path to follow, and that path will be based on some single notion of reality and faith which is based on one pre-existing notion of religion.

Well, if you are waiting for the one true path to the future to be written on these pages, you are waiting in vain. Or not.

Since any representation of the whole, all-that-is, will only be partial, then it follows that any path toward a single representation will only be partial ... or only one of many, many paths. If I take you deep into the woods on a dewy morning of summer, I can probably show you a giant spider web across the trail between several trees. If I ask you to show me the path from the center to the outside of the web, you can show me a path ... but watch as I jiggle the edge of the web just a little but (like an insect landing) at the point on the outside you choose. The spider will, in all likelihood, take a different path than the one you opted for. And if I do it again, another path. From the center to the edge there are many, many paths (and just as many from the edge to the center!). And that is only one web out of many, many in that one forest. And that forest is only one out of many, many in that county. And so ... always many paths.

And when we are speaking of ultimates, like all-that-is, the number of paths to its center from where we are spiritually is infinite. No one path more "the" path than another, *except* for the one path that speaks to you, which is your path.

So, I cannot tell you your path.

But I can suggest several paths through the qualities of spirited faith that might awaken in you the one you need to travel at this time. I am not saying any one of these is "the path", or even "your path"; only that in thinking about this question, in adding in your own queries, you will come closer to the path you need to be on than by taking anyone else's path.

And lest you worry that this means it will be a very lonely journey along your own path, if you are actively looking for connections not differences, then it is very likely you will find your path and the paths of other to coincide for much or all of your own journey in this life.

Randolph W.B. Becker

≈ ≈ ≈≈ ≈ ≈

One path would be to consider the ten elements of faith as a hierarchy – one thing following another. Each one building on the ones that have gone before. Like a giant staircase you are ascending toward the pinnacle of meaning or descending toward the depth of understanding.

On this path, you will probably find some of the early steps easy. Wow, this doesn't feel like work at all. I know all of this. I have learned and remembered all of this. This is second nature to me now.

But then there will come a step which gets a little harder. Omph! This takes some work. It feels familiar, but I still have to think a bit about making my faith evident in my living.

And then comes the step that you can't make. It feels foreign, too hard. You don't feel like you have a firm footing on the step below to allow you to step up this high. And it is a little frightening up this high, away from what seems so familiar.

And ahead, you can barely, if at all, make out the next steps.

If this is how you see your path into the future, then you know where you have work to do. You know that at those steps where the going gets tough, the "what now" is challenging you. You know the starting place of your path, you can see how it is headed, but you cannot see where it is headed ultimately. It will take faith in the path being yours to assure you that you are headed in your direction.

Does this sound like how you would like to explore

your path through these concepts?

If so, then for those steps which challenge you but which feel possible, for those concepts you need to be learning and remembering, focus on those chapters in this book. Look as well to other books and sources (there are some links in the epilogue) that speak to these growing points. This book, for such a path, becomes a set of guided tours to be taken in order.

And recognize that it will be hard going. Nothing worth getting to comes without some effort. Focusing this intently on one step of the process, and focusing on the spiritual, is not easy.

Do you think you are up to that? Good.

You have found your "now what!"

≈ ≈ ≈≈ ≈ ≈

Another path would be to decide to look holistically at the values of a reclaimed, spirited faith. To understand that no one of them stands alone. Indeed, as one becomes more spiritual, which might seem like an endpoint, that very spirituality will show one how to be even more radically open, connected, unitary, etc.

Maybe your path is to see that you cannot isolate or prioritize the values ... it is more of a globe than a staircase, in which the skin of the globe centers on what we would call spirited faith, and without some sense of holism there is no globe and is no center. Therefore, this is a path of moving about in ever-entwining circles, like trying to cover a large balloon with toilet paper ... to get it done and to stay you have to go over each part of the balloon many times, from many directions.

If this sounds like how you move to meaning, going to and fro, from many perspectives, covering the same territory until you know it as your own, then this could be your path. It would lead you to start with whichever of the ten values speaks to you at any moment, and then to wherever you feel called to proceed from there. Maybe you think about being "hopeful" in your faith, and that leads you to consider how such faith is "freeing", maybe it leads you to think about how to be "creative" in your response to trying times. This book, for such a path, is more like a supply closet – here's your balloon, your toilet paper, and some glue. How you use it is up to you, and how much you get out of it depends on how you use it. But just remember, when you have woven the fabric around the balloon comprehensively, solidly, wisely, the balloon can disappear and what you have learned (the toilet paper) will remain (be remembered) to always provide a guiding circle to your faith. It takes patience, perseverance, and desire.

Does this sound like you? Good.
You have found your "now what!"

≈ ≈ ≈≈ ≈ ≈

Another path would not appear to be path except in retrospect. I would call it the smorgasbord approach. Sometime watch what happens at a smorgasbord or buffet. Some people, with everything imaginable available, will take a plate of food that exactly resembles an *ala carte* offering. They will serve themselves in predictable, standard courses. That is their path through the bounty of food.

But then there are others who move through the offerings with no apparent rhyme or reason. Some appetizers are gathered along with some dessert. Then, on a second go-around, three vegetables are supplemented by cheese and crackers. The third trip to the buffet yields an entree, some soup, and ice cream. And when asked, they say, "I took what appealed to me."

The equivalent in a faith path would be a person who gathers the elements together in whatever order appeals to them, believing that it is the sum total of the elements, not the order or the specific pathway through the elements that counts. Today they say they will think a bit about "contemplative," and another day "unitary". Some days, when they take "contemplative" it fills them up. Other days they can't digest it at all. Other days, it is like a light appetizer inviting them to delve deeper in some other area.

For such a person, this book would be one banquet table. In their ideal restaurant (from the word "to restore") of the soul would be many tables, not just this one. They would want to be surrounded by many different buffets ... many choices. Then, they could feast on the wealth of offerings. Their path would be to this book sometimes, for what appeals to them at the moment, and then to another source for what appeal to them there.

This is a hard path to follow too. One has to strive to find a balanced diet, one that nourishes as well as fills.

One has to be careful not to so focus on one dish, one course, one aspect, that there is no room for other desirables. But, with such diligent attention to spiritual nutrition, one might find a much wider menu than could be had by a linear or concentric understanding.

Does this sound like your path? Good!
You have found your "now what!"

≈ ≈ ≈≈ ≈ ≈

Another path is to consider it all like a journey. Not a guided tour type of journey, but a free-lance one. A person on this kind of path will have done a lot of preliminary preparation: read in many religious traditions, explore a number of spiritual disciplines, and so forth. But now, the time for travel has come.

At first, the journey goes off without a hitch. It is smooth sailing along the path. Just like those on guided tour, the ways seems easy. But then there comes a change on the pathway. Unknown in the preparation and without a specific tour guide along to handle the issues, the individual is left to find the way. Maybe it is the obstruction of a significant loss in an area where continuity had been presumed. Maybe it is only a diversion because a shining stream, not marked on the consulted maps, enticed one down a side trail but washed out the trail back. Maybe it is a fork in the road with both road being roads not taken. Maybe, in the darkness of a forest along the way, fear becomes more of a companion than had been expected. Maybe the joy of a sunrise along the way bid one to stop, sit, ponder, stay a while, whilst parts of the planned pathway ahead shifted in the morning light. Who knows?

To such a free-lance traveler who makes the highways and byways of faith their path, a few maps, some general guides become traveling companions. Not that they can construct reality to match their predictions, but that they can remind one of the general direction of one's journey. To such a person on such a path, the chapters of this book become reminders of the intent of the journey toward reclaimed personal faith. They do not as much turn to the ideas to find out where they are as to remember what they were about when they lost their way or had their way blocked.

This is also a hard path (what path is not?) for it is a path of continuing personal interpretations and choices. Even the best prior planning can only take one so far down the path before life intervenes in ways unpredictable. This path requires both courage and wisdom – the courage to choose and the wisdom to know when to turn back to familiar sources to renew direction.

Does this sound like your path? Good!
You have found your "now what!"

≈ ≈ ≈≈ ≈ ≈

Another path is to see this book as a resource, not a map or a guide. Like a great cookbook, these chapters represent combinations of the ingredients of identity, experience, insight, learning, and spirit which can be combined in numerous ways to create sustaining, soulful faith.

Randolph W.B. Becker

Those who like to cook, not just follow recipes, will know this path. It is an adventuresome path. It is risky. Sometimes bread fails to rise. Sometimes the combination only sound good in theory, but not in the mouth. What is delicious in one culture is too bland or too spicy in another.

The joy of this path is not just in the eventually dish (faith) prepared that proves nourishing and delicious, but also in the preparation. The path is as meaningful as the meal.

This book, for such a path, becomes a series of recipes, from which to choose a meal, and each meal chosen may be different, until you sense that you are setting the menu, the table, and even the ingredients more than this book is doing it for you. Eventually you will not even need this book, but sometimes, when you want something familiar, or you want to start on a new tack, then you return to these recipes. For this path, you read these chapters over and over until they are yours, yours to the extent that you can innovate from them to new delights.

And, yes, it is hard to do that. It takes daring. And a lot of self-confidence. And an ability to deal with failure. But, it is also a path on which no one will ever accuse you of having a "fast food" faith.

Does this sound like your path? Good!
You have found your "now what!"

≈ ≈ ≈≈ ≈ ≈

And most likely, as you have read this book, and now

as you have read these descriptions of different faith paths, you have said to yourself, "I think my faith path is more like ..."

Like what?

If you had to speak of your path in a similar set of paragraphs, what would you say. What analogies would you use?

Would you see using this book in the process along your path? How?

What would make your path hard?

What would be the special rewards for you?

The challenge is not that you need to be on one of the paths I have chosen to describe, but that you choose to be on a path that you can describe.

You need to know what it looks like for you.

You need to know what the challenges of that path are likely to be.

You need to know what rewards you can reasonably expect.

You need to know what resources you will need to help you along the way.

As I write this, I am reminded that all of the great spiritual leaders of all time have had to deal with the same issues. No matter who they were, what times they lived in, how spiritually complete they may have seemed, they were each on their own unique path. They had to know how to describe that path in terms they could understand. The had to be honest about the challenges and rewards. They had to know the sources of their own strength, so they could rely on those resources in times of need.

Religions grew by institutionalizing those wise women's and men's answers to their own questions about their own paths of faith. But their personal faith grew out of their own questions!

We began our exploration with a simple question:

Is this really "life as we know it?"

In responding, you found that the question had validity, had meaning, for you.

From that simple question, we have followed a path through many questions.

Along the way we have explored a number of ways to consider those questions. I have offered few if any answers, hoping the answers would come to, through, and from you. And that has been the intent of this book, to help all of us to look at how to focus, how to proceed, and which of the paths to the future we will choose as our own.

The choice is ever yours –
to live on a path created out of the answers of others
or
on a path created out of the questions of your own soul.

One path leads to religion, and the other to your faith.

Epilogue

Spiritual persistence

One of the questions I am ironically asked when I speak about the message in this book is, "What answers have you found?"

Part of me wants to say, right out front, "This is not about the answers I have found, but about the questions you need to ask."

But another part of me wants to share the faith I have found when I have been open to living these values.

Why do I want to share what I have found?

Of course, I think there is value in my faith. And I think that some of the value I find for myself might spark some value in you, the reader. Not that you would follow, lock-step, in my value footprints, but that you would open your eyes that much wider by seeing what is valuable to me. As I suggested in Chapter 9, one of the best methods I have found to be creative in one's faith is to be open to the faith paths of others; look for connections.

There is another reason, as well, that I will share my faith path with you. We, especially in western culture, have followed a single notion about spirituality for millennia. A variant of this single theme is also pervasive in eastern religion as well. I want to suggest that this theme has not only kept us from seeing other possibilities, it has led us down a cul-de-sac of faith rather than along an open path.

Reclaiming the Sould of Your Faith

In sharing one vision of how we move back from dead end to open pathway, I hope I will inspire in your mind and spirit your own way of expressing a similarly more open understanding of life, spirit, and faith.

The unifying theme in almost all of the world's religions is that we each are on independent, disconnected journeys of spiritual existence. In its most stark form, represented in Christian theology, you have a pre-existence in which you are part of the divine or flow from the divine, you then move into physical existence for a single lifetime, and finally you move into an eternal spiritual existence, perhaps with but not part of the divine. One pre-life, one life, one after-life.

In the eastern version of this notion, you were spun out of the divine, you may have had many past lives, trying to work out your own karma and darma, destiny and spiritual baggage, so that at last you can find bliss in a fulfillment of your spiritual self. One pre-life, many lives, one ultimate after-life.

In each of these versions of the same spiritual understanding, humanity (or physical life) is bound on the one side by a creative event out of the divine, and bound on the other side by some level of eternal spiritual existence, but not a return into the divine. In between, whether in one or more lives, one is trying to work out some level of deficiencies. How well one does that determines either the nature of the eternal spiritual existence or the number of physical manifestations until that spiritual existence is achieved.

And each spirit, soul, person, is doing that alone.

Ideas like salvation, redemption, restoration, and the like, all talk about individual spiritual paths. And they speak about those paths occurring only in the space bounded by the human physical and spiritual experience. Ultimates are reduced to a very narrow range of possibility. (I am reminded, once again, of the reduction of the infinite to a small circle, and then the projection of that circle as if it were the infinite.)

What could be one alternative?

Let me spin out a narrative for you, which shares in concrete symbols some of the notions I hold in faith. See if this vision resonates with you.

All-that-is, the sum total of existence, has always included what you call "you" in it. But, the "you" that you know now has not always been the same manifestation.

At some point, spiritual energy/matter (it is impossible, at its essence, to differentiate between the two) of the most primitive nature became contained within all-that-is, but began its own distinct path.

Like a single celled animal, or a simple sub-atomic particle, an identity arose for some portion of all-that-is. Not an identity separate from all-that-is, but within it.

To continue to have that separate identity, the spiritual entity had to express itself, find its own fulfillment. Through a number of spiritual experiences, the entity had to learn and remember what it was about.

Once that entity knew, really knew and remembered, incorporated that identity into itself, it then had two distinct features ... its own identity and its ability to combine with other entities to form something more complex. By coming into an incorporated knowledge of its identity, the entity could find union outside of itself.

So, a more complex level of spiritual entities came into being, the result of simpler spiritual entities connecting.

Now, picture if you will, an infinite progression of such spiritual fulfillments, each producing a more complex spiritual entity out of less complex spiritual entities that continue to remember their basic spiritual natures.

That string of spiritual complexity would contain within it the combined learnings and rememberings of each of the its constituent parts ... spiritually, what existed in simplest form persists in each level of growing complexity; just as the nature of sub-atomic particles is retained even as we view the resultant atomic whole.

From the simplest level of differentiation within all-that-is, an infinite number of fulfillments and connections have created infinitely more complex spiritual entities. And, at last, that process reaches the spiritual level in which we now exist. More complex than many entities, less complex than many entities. On the infinite journey between initial differentiation and ultimate connection with all of all-that-is, we are infinitely in the middle.

So, where does that leave us?

It means that we as spiritual beings are the more complex combinations of less complex spiritual entities.

We, through a series of physical and spiritual experiences (lives and not-lives, if you will), seek to find an understanding of our nature as spiritual entities. We are provided with enough lives to learn and really remember what we need in order to be wholly, understandably, and expressively what we are spiritually. Enough go-arounds that we are capable of making meaningful, sustained connections with other spiritual entities of this level of complexity. We connect in order to move on in the process of spiritual enhancement and spiritual persistence.

Each of us has a different task before us. We each need to learn and remember what it means to be "us" spiritually. It does us no good to try to learn what it means to be someone else, or what it means in general. We each have our own fulfillment to find.

BUT

we cannot move into a more complex spiritual entity by ourselves. Just as hydrogen combining with hydrogen does not give you anything more complex than hydrogen, we being fulfilled simply achieve the full potential of the spiritually persistent entity that we are, but we do not become more complex in the process. Much may be fulfilled, but nothing is enhanced.

We need connection with other fulfilled spiritual entities at our same level of complexity in order to move into more complex, enhanced spiritual existence.

Ultimately, then, life (or lives) is not about finding our own individual salvation, but rather about finding ourselves so we can join with others to move along this path of spiritual persistence and enhancement.

We are not, and cannot be in this just for ourselves. If we try, we stop moving toward greater complexity, and stop moving toward a union with the totality of all-that-is.

We also stop the enhancement of all-that-is if we try to be in this just for ourselves. If all-that-is is shaped by the infinite spiritual entities within it, then our failure to move into meaningful connection denies the whole some portion of potential enhancement and fulfillment.

In this view of our spiritual nature (we are more spiritual beings having periodic physical experiences than physical beings who occasionally have spiritual experiences), ultimately there is no loss. Nothing which ever existed spiritually is lost even as it is combined into more complex entities. The simplest is always resident in the very essence of the more complex. Talk about a notion of after-life! All that arises from here on will include the "us" of now within the enhanced structure, not as differentiated identity but as a part of its incorporated spiritual essence.

Of course, this faith of mine is more complex than is outlined here. At the end of this epilogue, I will share with you some other sources if you want to explore these concepts in more depth because they seem to awaken some understandings and appreciations in you.

But, given this outline, let me show you how this faith works within the ten values of spiritual faith of this book.

OPEN - to be anything other than open, I may be closing off the spiritual experiences and/or the spiritual connections I need for my spiritual fulfillment and enhancement. In fact, I cannot tell on the surface of human behavior whether the person most like me or the person who seems most unlike me may hold the piece I will need to form a meaningful connection into greater complexity. If I am not open, with a view to being inclusive, I may be shutting out the very learning I need to remember. So, a radical openness is a requirement.

CONNECTED - since the ultimate mode of this faith is connection, I certainly need to look for all the points of connection that I can find. In trying to go it alone, to find any differentiated or individualistic path, I would be working against my own spiritual enhancement.

UNITARY- while I may be having a seemingly individualized experience at a given moment, Spiritual Persistence reminds me that all is moving through connection toward a unified end, and such motion is always occurring within all-that-is. You cannot connect outside of that whole. The questions are: how much of that whole am I connected to at my present level of spiritual complexity and how can I connect to more?

HOPEFUL - With the assurance that all the constituent less-complex entities persist in my present spiritual reality, I know that I retain as a foundation all the assembled and connected remembered learnings. I have no need to look backwards. What is important from "back there" is remembered in the simple fact of my spiritual existence. So, I can focus on the tasks at hand that will open the future to me. And, I am also assured that the future which will come, will be along the path toward more connection with all the other elements of all-that-is.

FREEING - I find it infinitely freeing to have the horizon be infinite. If I retain all that has come before along the path that has created me spiritually, and if what I now experience as a spiritual identity will be retained into all the connections ahead, then I am free to be open to all those learnings that may inform me toward my fulfillment. I am not confined to one particular mode of thought. If there is no one, single, "right" path from simplicity to ultimate complexity and connection, then I am freed to explore many, seeking to find the one that will be most appropriate to the "me" that has been spiritually created by prior connection.

CONTEMPLATIVE - Think of our constituent spiritual elements as the "answers" we already have. Functioning like spiritual traits, these foundations do not need to be rediscovered or redeemed. So, I am freed to follow my questions rather than seek what are seen as essential answers. The things I need to know to be "me" are already known. My questions point the way to how that "me" will be able to find connection with other entities, to grow in spiritual complexity.

INDEPENDENT - In one sense, I am not independent; I have been shaped by those entities whose connection has meant my spiritual existence. But now, at this spiritual level, my challenge is to shape what I have been given in ways that will make possible further, more-complex connections. If I rely on the institutions of culture, if I rely on the directions given by others, then I will not be shaping what I need to shape. To be influenced in that way would be to forsake the very essence of the challenge of spiritual existence ... to fulfill my spirit. If I do allow myself to be more influenced that to influence, I will be given as many life opportunities as it takes until I find I can remember to shape, not be shaped.

CREATIVE - The learning, and the remembering, that will be necessary to move into connection will not come simply to me by my sitting and waiting for it to occur. It is not a matter of revelation, but of interaction. I need to find those ways in which I can use my spiritual energy, awareness, and potential to enhance, to fulfill what I received by being.

ACCESSIBLE-REASONABLE - I find it evident that there is nothing that can exist separate from all-that-is, and that all-that-is cannot exist without everything, including me. I find it evident that nothing which once was is ever lost to existence, although it may be incorporated in other ways. I find that all of this can be explained in simple language, in terms I can use and explain. All the pieces fit without any mystery or secrets.

SPIRITUAL - Nothing in these concepts requires one to locate any of the process in specific material reality. Each person, in his/her many lives, is many different people who turn to many different sources of inspiration, who use many different languages and symbols. Nothing material has any abiding presence in our spiritual being. And in connecting into a more complex spiritual entity, we connect spiritually, not materially. This is not about mating, but about connecting ... not creating a "thing" separate from us, but coming to exist within a shared awareness.

That is how Spiritual Persistence works for me.
Perhaps this way of looking at one's faith is helpful to

you, offering a new vantage point on faith, one that does not share the usual limitations of prevailing religions.

Perhaps not.

If it is helpful, at the end of this Epilogue you will find an invitation.

If it is not helpful, then what would be helpful to you in shaping your faith?

What would your faith structure look like if you had to describe it as I have described mine?

Are there points at which yours and mine connect?

For me, the bottom line is that we, at this level of spiritual complexity, will not find one, single, supreme way of understanding spiritual evolution and personal faith that will fit everyone, answer every question, and contain all truth.

Rather, it is that we look for ways to think, understand, and know our faith by which:

> our experience of living is revealed in our questions,
> our experience of questioning is responded to with evermore inclusive answers,
> and our experience with those answers is remembered in the very fabric of our living.

That is the soul of my faith, which I have reclaimed.

≈≈≈

Randolph W.B. Becker

An Invitation

To explore more of the concepts outlined in this Epilogue, I invite you to be in touch with me at:

nextsteps@spiritualpersistence.com.

About the Author

Randolph W.B. Becker has spent his professional career as a Unitarian Universalist Minister and a spiritual adventurer. He has taught at several colleges and theological schools and had one of the first podcasts on a religious theme as the Internet developed. When pressed for a definition, he claims to be a "spiritual humanist."

The New Atlantian Library

NewAtlantianLibrary.com or
AbsolutelyAmazingeBooks.com
or AA-eBooks.com

www.ingramcontent.com/pod-product-compliance
Lightning Source LLC
Chambersburg PA
CBHW050803160426
43192CB00010B/1627